HITTING

HITTING

by Jay Feldman

Little Simon / **Published by Simon & Schuster**

NEW YORK / LONDON / TORONTO / SYDNEY / TOKYO / SINGAPORE

A BASEBALL INK BOOK

The views expressed in this book are solely
those of the author and do not necessarily represent
those of Major League Baseball®.

The Major League Baseball® trademarks are used
with the permission of Major League Baseball Properties, Inc.

Photo credits appear on page 88.

LITTLE SIMON
Simon & Schuster Building
Rockefeller Center
1230 Avenue of the Americas
New York, NY 10020

Copyright © 1991 by Professional Ink, Inc.

Also available in a SIMON & SCHUSTER BOOKS FOR YOUNG READERS
hardcover edition.

Manufactured in the United States of America
1 3 5 7 9 10 8 6 4 2

Library of Congress Cataloging-in-Publication Data

Feldman, Jay. Hitting.
(An Official major league baseball® book)
Summary: Teaches the art and science of hitting a baseball
in a comprehensive manner, including practice exercises. 1. Batting
(Baseball) — Juvenile literature. [1. Batting (Baseball) 2. Baseball.] I. Title. II. Series.
GV869.F45 1991 796.357'26 — dc20 90-41356
ISBN 0-671-73318-4
ISBN 0-671-70442-7 (pbk)

To my father Ben, for his patience,

my older son Blue Jay, for his talent,

and my younger son Ben, for his promise.

ACKNOWLEDGMENTS

I'd like to thank the following people: Dusty Baker, for his time and patience with my endless questions, and for his friendship over the years; Harold Baines, Wade Boggs, Andre Dawson, Carney Lansford, and Ryne Sandberg, for their willingness to participate in this project and for freely sharing their knowledge; public relations directors John Blake (Texas Rangers), Richard Bresciani (Boston Red Sox), Ned Colletti (Chicago Cubs), and Kathy Jacobson (Oakland Athletics) for their perseverance in arranging interviews; University of California, Davis, varsity baseball coach Phil Swimley, for his clear explanations of theory, and for his help with my own hitting; California Angels' scout Loyd Christopher, for his enthusiasm, and for the tips he passed along; my very good friend James Rodewald of *Sports Illustrated*, for his research help; our player models, Erik Schirmer, Katrina Wamsley, Michael Onyon, Danielle Schleede, Stephen Whitaker, and Stephen Williams; and finally, my wife Marti, for her love, support, and faith in me.

Jay Feldman

AUTHOR'S NOTE

Nowadays more and more girls are playing baseball. As a person who both loves baseball and believes in equality, I find this trend exciting and hopeful. Since this book is for young ballplayers, male and female alike, I've tried to use sex-neutral language as much as possible in addressing the reader. The English language hasn't always supported this effort.

In order to provide in-depth advice to young players, I decided to concentrate my interviews on a select group of hitters who have demonstrated success over the years. In addition, I felt it important to include the advice of one major league hitting instructor. Accordingly, much of the personal advice in this book comes from my first-hand interviews with five players (Harold Baines, Wade Boggs, Andre Dawson, Carney Lansford and Ryne Sandberg) and one batting coach (Dusty Baker). I chose these hitters for several reasons: they all combine power and average; three are National Leaguers (Baker, Dawson and Sandberg) and three American Leaguers (Baines, Boggs and Lansford); four bat righthanded (Baker, Dawson, Lansford and Sandberg) and two lefthanded (Baines and Boggs).

In addition to those six players, I have also used quotes from other players which were taken from other sources.

Finally, a reminder: *in all instances of playing or practicing, wear a protective batting helmet.*

CONTENTS

CHAPTER 1

A Brief History of Hitting Instructionals

Hitting has been a topic for study since baseball began. Perhaps the simplest, truest statement on the subject was made by Wee Willie Keeler, who played in the major leagues from 1892 to 1910, banging out 2,947 base hits and finishing his career with a .343 lifetime batting average. Keeler summed up his approach to hitting as follows: "Hit 'em where they ain't."

From Wee Willie Keeler's time on, batting secrets have been passed from coaches to players, and from one player to another. Over the years some of the accepted knowledge about hitting has been accurate, and some has not.

Among the false notions about hitting which were handed down from one generation to the next were the ideas that (1) you hit off your back leg, and (2) you roll your wrists at the moment of contact. It has only been in recent years that these misleading ideas have been proven untrue.

Many instructional books provided very little in the way of useful information. The most helpful thing one early book advises is to "clench your teeth, watch the ball, and when it passes you step into it."

In addition, batting instruction books have reflected the style of play which was current at the time they were written. For example, future Hall of Famer John McGraw, a very good player and one of the greatest managers in history, recommends the following in his 1914 book *How to Play Baseball*: "The best style is to 'choke' the bat up short and use a chop swing." McGraw was a product of an era in which heavy, thick-handled bats and a "dead ball" made this hitting technique advisable.

Many hitting instructionals create misleading impressions. In 1951 Enos Slaughter, another future Hall of Famer, wrote: "If you are facing a pitcher who has a blazing fastball, you should start your swing the moment the ball leaves his hand. At that moment you begin your stride, your grip begins to tighten, and you start bringing the bat around." This creates the impression that the stride and the swing should begin at the same time, which is not true.

The main problem with those early instruction books was that none of them really examined the mechanics of hitting in detail.

Wee Willie Keeler, who used an enormous bat to "hit 'em where they ain't."

Ted Williams, one of the greatest hitters of all time and the author of The Science of Hitting.

John McGraw, whose advice to young hitters in 1914 was to "'choke' the bat up short and use a chop swing."

Charlie Lau, whose theories on hitting have been adopted by many current major league players and batting instructors.

Kansas City's George Brett is perhaps the most celebrated disciple of the Charlie Lau school of hitting.

In 1970 former Boston Red Sox star Ted Williams wrote *The Science of Hitting*, the first serious study to break hitting down into its separate parts and explain the fundamentals of each part.

Williams was one of the greatest hitters baseball has ever known. In 1941 he hit .406, the last time anyone has topped the magical .400 mark. He ended his playing career in 1960, at the age of 42, hitting .316 in his last season. During his career, he won six American League batting championships, four home run crowns, and four RBI titles.

Williams had a lifetime batting average of .344, with 2,654 hits, 521 home runs, and 1,839 runs batted in. His totals are all the more impressive when you realize that he missed five seasons during his prime. (He was a fighter pilot in the Armed Services for three years during World War II and

served two more years during the Korean War.)

In *The Science of Hitting*, Williams says, "If there is such a thing as a science in sport, hitting a baseball is it. As with any science, there are fundamentals, certain tenets of hitting every good batter or batting coach could tell you. But it is not an exact science. Much of it has been poorly defined, or not defined at all, and some things have been told wrong for years."

In addition to stressing the importance of your hips leading your hands, Williams was especially insistent on pointing out that your top hand does *not* roll upon contact.

The next major contribution to the study of hitting was made by Charlie Lau, who wrote *The Art of Hitting .300* in 1980. Lau had been an average player—his lifetime batting average was .255—but he had the good fortune to play on teams with some great hitters. In the course of his major league career, he was a teammate of such stars as Al Kaline, Harvey Kuenn, Hank Aaron, Eddie Mathews, and Frank Robinson, and he studied them carefully.

After retiring as a player, Lau became a manager and a hitting instructor. In his study of hitting, he used a technique which had not been possible in an earlier era. He watched ultra-slow-motion films and videotapes of hundreds of hitters and noticed that most of the good ones did certain things in a similar fashion.

The films revealed things that the naked eye could not see, and Lau became convinced that some important principles of hitting which had been accepted and taught for many years were simply not accurate. In particular, Lau disagreed strongly with the idea that you hit off your back leg, and like Williams, he taught that the top hand doesn't roll on contact.

As hitting instructor for the Kansas City Royals in the late seventies, Lau played an important role in the success of the Royals teams of that era. One of Lau's most brilliant pupils was Kansas City Royals star George Brett, whose hitting mastery helped popularize Lau's method. In 1980 Brett hit a monstrous home run into the third deck at Yankee Stadium off relief pitcher Goose Gossage to clinch the final game of the American League Championship Series. In the locker room after the game, on national TV, Brett was shown the videotape of the blast, and asked him to comment. His joyful response was "Thank you, Charlie Lau."

After leaving the Royals, Lau worked for the New York Yankees and Chicago White Sox, influencing such stars as Reggie Jackson, Lou Piniella, Carlton Fisk, and Harold Baines. Lau's second book, *The Winning Hitter*, was published in 1984, the same year he died.

Ted Williams called hitting a "science," and Charlie Lau called it an "art," but they both stressed the importance of discipline and hard work.

Hitting is both a science and an art. Like a scientist, you must study the theory and the fundamental principles, and then apply them in a systematic way. But like an artist, as you master the proper mechanics and techniques, you begin to bring your own style to them.

Make no mistake about it—an artist must work as hard as a scientist. As the great American inventor Thomas Edison said, "Genius is one percent inspiration, and ninety-nine percent perspiration."

Nobody can get by on talent alone. Study and practice are the keys to success, whether the field is science, art or hitting. Hall of Famer Rogers Hornsby, whose lifetime batting average of .358 is the second highest in baseball history, said, "A great hitter isn't born, he's made. He's made out of practice, fault correction and confidence."

Learning to hit is a three-step process. First, you must understand the theory. Second, you must practice the mechanics properly. Third, you must apply them when you come to the plate in a game.

This book points the way. The rest is up to you.

Batting tips from the Babe

Before you go on to read what today's top batters have to say about the art and science of hitting, here are a few words of wisdom from the greatest of them all, the one and only Sultan of Swat. His advice is excerpted from an early instructional titled Babe Ruth's Own Book of Baseball; *published in 1928, the Bambino's words are as valuable today as they were then.*

No ballplayer ever made good either as a hitter or a fielder unless he had well developed wrist and forearm muscles. There are a lot of exercises that can be used to get that development.

One of the most common methods used by ballplayers to strengthen the wrist and forearm is to carry around a rubber ball all the time and squeeze it. If you do that for fifteen or twenty minutes a day you can strengthen your forearm a lot—and if you don't think those muscles get a real workout by gripping, just try it. The first fif-

Babe Ruth is well-known for his 714 home runs, but he also put together a .342 lifteime batting average, good enough to make him the tenth highest of all time.

teen minutes of that exercise will make your arm ache clear to the elbow.

One of the most common faults of kid hitters particularly is that they don't use the proper bat. Most of them try to swing bats that are too heavy, figuring of course that the heavier the bat, the more distance they can get. That's wrong. Any time a player uses a bat that feels heavy in his hands, he's making a mistake. The ideal bat is one that balances perfectly, one that can be swung with the same easy, smooth motion with which you swing your arms. A bat that's too heavy requires a jerk to start on its way, and once under way it requires additional effort to direct its course. Naturally, that makes a jerky, choppy swing, and that's not so good,

All hitters have different styles. But there are certain features in which all hitters—if they're good ones—act alike.

They all have perfect balance, perfect timing, and a good eye. Balance and timing are much the same. It is timing which enables a batter to meet the ball at the exact instant when all their body is thrown into the swing. It's timing which enables a batter to hit fast and slow balls with equal ease. It's timing which, more than any one thing, is the secret of real hitting.

And the unfortunate thing about it is that timing is one thing which you just can't teach. It's born into you. You either have it or you don't.

Next time you go to a ballgame, watch the really great hitters. You'll notice that they don't seem to swing any harder, or with any longer arc, than the poor hitters. But they have perfect timing sense. That's the most important thing in batting.

As I said before, a person either has a sense of timing or they don't. But you can improve your timing. Lots of times I went into slumps, as do all other hitters. The first thing I looked to was my timing. I tried to swing a bit later or a bit earlier. I shortened or lengthened my stride. I experimented with every angle of timing. And usually I corrected my fault, even though I may not know exactly what it is.

And the ability to get out of a slump is another test of a real hitter. Some fellows claim that a slump doesn't bother them, that they take it as a matter of course, knowing that they will work out of it sooner or later. That's bunk. There never was a ballplayer who lived who could go through a batting slump without worrying. It's simply a question of how much you worry, and whether or not your worry is about the slump or over methods of overcoming it.

The worst part of a batting slump is that it affects your play in the field, too. As long as the basehits are coming regularly, the average ballplayer is sitting on top of the world. He has pepper and enthusiasm. Everything is fine. But when the old slump comes along everything is upside down.

With me, I've found that the best method of overcoming a slump is to choke up on my bat and start "choke hitting" for a while. I reduce my stride to a minimum and I "push" instead of "pull" the ball. And most of all, I try to worry as little as possible about it.

Sometimes when I was in a slump I'd catch myself tightening up with the pitch. When I did that I would simply call for time, and step out of the box until I could get squared around and loosened up again. As a result of the anxiety, you're more apt to swing at bad balls simply because you're too anxious to hit.

CHAPTER 2

One Tough Job

It's been said many times, and you may have heard it before: *Hitting a baseball is the single most difficult feat in sports.*

Is it true? And if so, why?

Consider this: the very best hitters don't succeed more than three or four times out of ten tries—a 30 to 40 percent success rate. In what other team sport would that be an acceptable standard? In football the great quarterbacks complete between 50 and 60 percent of their passes. In basketball the best shooters hit 50 to 60 percent from the floor and 85 to 95 percent from the foul line.

Even in baseball the acceptable success rate for hitting is far below that of other categories of achievement. No pitcher, for example, would be considered effective if he threw only 30 to 40 percent of his pitches for strikes, and it's unthinkable that a fielder would only catch three or four out of every ten balls hit to him.

To understand why hitting a baseball can be so difficult, start by thinking about the size and shape of both the ball and the bat. The ball is a sphere, and the hitting surface of the bat is round. The diameter of the ball is about the same size as the diameter of the barrel of the bat. In other words, if you look at a cross section of each, you see two circles roughly the same size.

For the bat to make solid contact with the ball, it has to strike it pretty much center-to-center. The margin for error is very small. If the bat hits the ball near its top or bottom, you foul it back. If you hit it below the center, you pop it up. Above the center, it's a ground ball.

Not only do you have to hit it center-to-center in order to make solid contact, you also have to hit the ball so that its flight path carries it into fair territory. You can hit the ball hard, but if you've swung too early, you'll pull it foul (past first base if you're a lefthanded hitter, past third if you're a righty). If you're late with your swing, the ball will land outside the opposite foul line (past third base for lefties, past first for righthanded batters).

Another factor is what we refer to as the "fat part" of the bat, or the "sweet spot." Aluminum bats, of course, have a greater area of sweet spot than wooden ones but even an aluminum bat has its

Cross sections of a baseball and the barrel of a bat reveal two circles about the same size.

limitations. If you hit the ball either on the handle or too far up toward the top end, you'll rarely make solid contact.

But all these things wouldn't make it nearly so tough if it weren't for one other consideration: the ball is moving. As a batter you have to judge the flight of the ball as it approaches the plate, time it, and react—all in a split second. You have to decide whether the pitch is a fastball or a breaking ball, whether it's going to be in the strike zone, and if so, whether the game situation makes it a pitch you want to swing at.

And once you decide all that, you must then put the fat part of the bat center-to-center on the ball.

Compare this with a couple of other sports in which the player hits a ball. In golf, for example, the hitting surface of the club is larger than the ball, it's flat, and the ball is sitting still. In tennis the racket surface is also flat and much larger than the ball.

Clearly, the task of hitting a baseball has a set of unique, built-in problems which makes it one tough job. The single most difficult feat in sports? Maybe, maybe not. But one thing is certain: *Hitting a baseball solidly and consistently into fair territory is one of the most difficult feats in sports.*

Does all this mean you are defeated before you start? Not at all. The basic principles of hitting are known, and they can be learned. *You* can learn to be a successful hitter by following the principles explained in this book.

If you swing too early, you pull the ball foul. If you swing too late, it'll foul the other way.

If you hit the ball near the top or bottom, you'll foul it back. If you hit it below the center, it's a popup. If you hit it above the center, it's a ground ball.

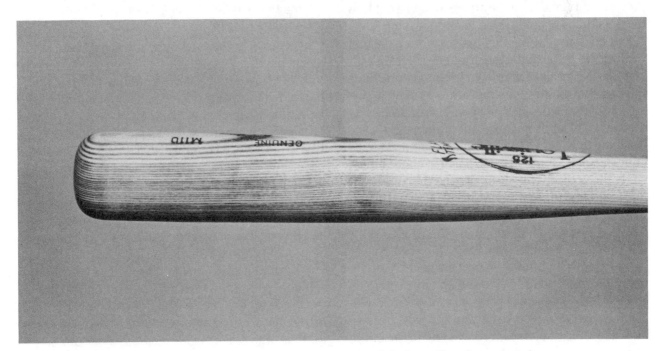

For solid contact, you want to hit the ball on the sweet spot of the bat. Aluminum bats have a larger sweet spot than wooden ones.

But if you want to be a good hitter, you must be willing to put in the time and effort it takes to become one. There are no shortcuts and no magic formulas. There are only three ways to get there: (1) practice, (2) practice, and (3) more practice.

And you must practice the correct principles. As former big league star and current San Francisco Giants' hitting instructor Dusty Baker says, "You have to repeat the movements to establish the 'muscle memory.' That is, you have to train your muscles to react in the proper way."

You can't simply go down to the batting cage, take a hundred whacks at the ball, and pat yourself on the back, thinking, "I've done my work for today." Because if you practice incorrectly, you'll be teaching your body bad habits, and you'll have to work doubly hard to correct them when you get older.

Don't make the mistake of thinking that because you may have some "natural" ability, you don't have to discipline yourself and learn the right methods. "There are a lot of guys," says Dusty Baker, "who have so much natural ability that they don't really think about some of the intricacies of hitting until they get hurt, and then they have to figure out how to adjust in order to be able to keep playing."

The best way to use this book is with a partner who will help you apply the principles, because it's very hard to analyze your own hitting habits. Even the pros have hitting instructors.

Try to find an older person—your father or mother, an older brother or sister, your coach—who is willing to work with you, or get a teammate to be your partner. You and your partner should each study the book, first individually and then together, until you both understand the principles. Then, when you are both confident that you grasp the basics, go out and start applying them.

If you know someone who has a video camera, try to get yourself filmed. This can be extremely helpful—when you see yourself on tape, you get a chance to observe your hitting as an outsider would. You can see your own strengths and weaknesses, and you can decide where you need to make changes.

Former major league star Dusty Baker, now the batting instructor for the San Francisco Giants.

In order to improve as a hitter, you must start with an open mind. You must be willing to try things you may not have tried before. You may have to abandon old ideas which you've had for a long time and be ready to adopt new ones.

In addition, you must have a positive attitude. You have to believe in your own ability to learn the skills of hitting, because whether or not you start with great "natural" talent, it is possible to improve by applying yourself.

Hitting is a mental and emotional discipline as well as a physical one. As Ted Williams says, "Hitting is 50 percent from the neck up." To be a good hitter, you have to train your mind as well as your body.

It doesn't matter whether you end up playing in the big leagues. Very few do. The important thing is to *make the most of your abilities*—develop them to their fullest, and *be the best hitter you can be.*

CHAPTER 3

Bats: Selection and Grip

Every job has its tools. An auto mechanic has a screwdriver and wrenches, a carpenter has a hammer and a saw, and a musician has an instrument. As a hitter, the tool of your trade is your bat.

Bats have changed quite a bit since the early days of baseball. The evolution of bats has been from heavy to light, from long to short, and from thick handles to thin ones.

With the heavier, thicker-handled bats used in the early days, the weight was more evenly distributed, and the bat was probably best swung with a short, chopping stroke. Wee Willie Keeler used a monstrous club to "hit 'em where they ain't."

In the 1920s, as the ball became livelier and Babe Ruth popularized power hitting, the handles slowly started to taper down, but bats were still long and heavy. The theory was that with a heavier bat you could hit the ball farther.

In the 1940s hitters like Ted Williams and Stan Musial showed that you could hit a ball just as far with a light bat, and players began using lighter sticks. The handles were still thick and the bats still long, however, compared to today's standards.

In the '50s and '60s many sluggers like Willie Mays and Ernie Banks swung light, long bats with good-sized handles.

In the '70s and '80s, with the increased emphasis on bat speed, handles got thinner and bats grew shorter as well as lighter.

Today most bats have extremely thin handles, which makes the barrel seem even bigger, because all the weight is at the hitting end. This makes it easier to whip the bat for power. In the case of wooden bats, it also causes them to snap above the handle more frequently. Aluminum bats don't break that way, but the thin-handle/thick-barrel combination encourages many young hitters to value power over contact. This can lead to bad hitting habits.

In choosing a bat, keep one thing in mind. Comfort. Regardless of the type of work, any professional will tell you that you have to feel comfortable with your tools. Hitting is no exception. You have to have a bat that feels good in your hands, that you can swing comfortably and with confidence. Only you can decide which bat you like best.

Jose Canseco relies upon the bat speed he can generate with a thin-handled model.

Darryl Strawberry (left) and Kevin Mitchell (right) are two sluggers who have proven that you can hit a ball just as far with a light bat as with a heavy one.

There are four things to consider: handle size, weight, length, and balance.

The right-sized handle is the one you can grip easily.

When it comes to weight, Ted Williams says, "I see no percentage at all in using a heavy bat. You can get the same result by being quicker with a light bat." This is sound advice—just make sure you don't get too light a bat or you won't get any punch behind your swing.

Again, when it comes to length, don't go for a bat that you'll have trouble getting around. Take one an inch shorter if necessary.

Balance, like handle size, is a matter of personal preference. Do you want a top-heavy bat or a more evenly weighted one?

It all comes down to what you like in a bat. All hitters agree that the number one factor with a bat is that you feel comfortable with it.

So now that you've chosen your bat, how do you hold it?

Over the years there have been various ideas about how to grip the bat. Everybody is different. The best idea is to grip the bat naturally and comfortably, somewhere around the meaty part of your hand—that is, somewhere between the hollow of your palm and the beginning of your fingers.

Keep your hands together. There was a time when batters commonly used a separated-hands grip, and some had great success with it. Hall of Famers Ty Cobb, who owns the highest lifetime batting average in history (.367), and Honus Wagner (.327 lifetime batting average), both used this technique. But since about 1930, nobody has used the separated-hands grip.

There *is* one very important thing about the grip: *don't squeeze the bat to death*, particularly when you're waiting for the pitch. Charlie Lau calls it the "white-knuckle syndrome," and it's the beginning of the end for a hitter. "The tension doesn't stay just in the hands," Lau points out. "It always works its way up, cording the muscles in the arms, tighten-

Big men like Carney Lansford (left) and Sal Bando (right) show that you don't have to be a "banjo hitter" to choke up on the bat.

ing up the shoulders, stiffening the neck, until the player is tense all over."

And the tension will creep into the worst place of all. The batter's mind. A tense mind and a tense body are the hitter's downfall.

So keep your hands relaxed. Your hands will instinctively tighten when you begin your stride.

The other thing you need to consider is where on the handle to hold the bat. Again, personal preference comes into play. Most players, like George Brett, and Wade Boggs, have their lower hand against the knob. Generally speaking, you can't go wrong with this position.

Some hitters prefer to choke up. Choking up can vary from an inch above the knob, like Carney Lansford, to several inches, like former Oakland A's captain Sal Bando. Choking up gives you more bat control, but you should only do it if it feels comfortable. If you usually hold the bat against the knob, you may want to try choking up when you have two strikes on you, in order to increase your bat control.

Some power hitters hang the little finger of their lower hand off the bat completely, in order to increase their leverage. This technique is not recommended for younger players because it results in a loss of bat control, and younger players should be concentrating on learning to make contact, not on power hitting.

Finally there is the issue of batting gloves. Again the answer is personal. Some hitters use one, some two, and some don't use any. Suit yourself—but if they don't feel good to you don't use them just because most of the big leaguers do.

Ty Cobb and Honus Wagner. Both separated their hands on the bat.

What the coach says

DUSTY BAKER The bat is just an extension of your arms. Make sure you have one that you're comfortable with.

What the hitters say

HAROLD BAINES I try to get a balanced bat. I use a smaller barreled bat. The most important thing is to be comfortable. I try not to grip the bat too tight. I don't want my top hand to be too dominant.

WADE BOGGS The big thing with bat selection is that the bat has to feel good in your hands. A lot of youngsters try to find a bat that everyone wants to use, and little kids wind up swinging big bats, and vice versa. You don't want

it too heavy and you don't want it too light. You want that perfect balance that feels good to you. One bat that might feel light to somebody else could be the bat that you should use. Just find the bat that's right for you.

I grip the bat where the fingers meet the palm. You don't want it too far back in your hand.

ANDRE DAWSON I think bat selection is one of the most important things about hitting. The bat should give you the confidence that you can drive the ball. It should feel good in your hands. I like a model that's not too heavy, not too light. Something I don't have to choke up on—I don't want to have to worry that the bat is going to swing me. I've seen some players use the grip with the pinky finger off the knob. I never even experimented with that, and I don't know how they can be effective with it.

CARNEY LANSFORD Use a bat that feels comfortable when you hold it. You don't want to get one too big or too small. Different batters like different type bats. I like one with a little bit thinner handle. Some guys like a thicker handle. It just depends on what feels comfortable to you. I try to keep the bat in my fingers. I don't want to get it too far back. I don't think about lining my knuckles up in any way.

EDDIE MURRAY I use a pretty light bat. I use a bat without a knob, and I feel really comfortable holding my hands all the way down at the bottom of the bat.

RYNE SANDBERG I think that picking the right bat is very important. I swing a fairly light bat. I just select the bat that feels comfortable, one that I feel I feel will allow me to keep my weight back and be quick if I have to. A bigger bat doesn't mean you're going to hit the ball farther. It's all in the bat speed. You want a bat you can swing quickly. One that you're comfortable with.

I try to line up the middle knuckles of one hand with the middle knuckles of the other hand, and I try to hold the bat in my fingers rather than in my palm, similar to a golf grip. I learned that way back. It's easier for me to swing that way, and it's easier to get my hands through.

CHAPTER 4

Contact Before Power

Everybody wants to be a hero. We've all dreamed of coming to bat in the last inning with the game on the line and belting a home run to win it.

Unfortunately there are a couple of problems with trying to hit home runs and be a hero. First of all, there's the emotional pressure you put on yourself. This type of pressure leads to physical tension, and tension is your worst enemy. Hitting is a difficult enough job—you don't need to create extra problems for yourself in this way.

The second problem is a physical one. Most of the time, if you want to hit a home run, you're going to be trying to pull the ball down the line because that's the closest place where you can hit it out. To do that, you've got to get just the right pitch (on the inside part of the plate), and you've got to tag it just right (at the earliest possible moment).

As a result you open up your hips and shoulders early, which pulls your head off the ball. If you get any other pitch than the one you're looking for, you seriously decrease your chances of hitting the ball. That's why so many power hitters strike out a lot.

Striking out is the worst at bat you can have as a hitter. Not only do you feel bad, but more than that, you haven't helped your team because you haven't even put the ball in play. If you hit a ground ball, at least there's a chance the infielder will kick it, and you'll wind up on first base. If you're on first, you've done your job. There may be more satisfying ways of getting there, but at least you're alive. If you score, the run doesn't count any less because you reached base on an error.

If you strike out with a runner on base, you've not only given up yourself, you've left the runner in place. If you put the ball in play, the runner has a chance to advance.

Let's say you come to bat with the score tied in the last inning of the ballgame. There's a runner on third and one out. The tension is intense. You get caught up in the excitement and start thinking about hitting a home run to win the game. As soon as you think that way, you've messed up. You don't need a home run to win the game. All you need is to bring that runner home from third. A ground ball to second base will do it. A fly ball to the outfield will do it. *Put the ball in play.* If you're swinging for the

If you're trying to pull the ball for a home run, it usually causes you to open up your hips and shoulders too soon and could pull your head off the ball. If you get any pitch other than the inside fastball you're hoping for, you seriously decrease your chances of contact.

fence and you strike out, your team will have two outs, and the options for bringing that runner home are much fewer.

You have to learn to hit the ball solidly and consistently into fair territory. And the only way to do that is to develop sound mechanics. If your mechanics are right, the power will come—you'll be surprised at how far you can hit the ball by focusing on mechanics and making contact.

What the coach says

DUSTY BAKER First of all, you can't really be looking to hit a home run in most cases. But if you are in a situation where you want to hit the ball out, I say try to hit to the big part of the ballpark if you have that kind of strength. If you're a little early, it's still fair, and if you're a little late, you can still hit it out if you have the power. Reggie Jackson told me he always looked to the big part of the park and waited for a pitch in his zone. But see, most guys that are trying to hit home runs are trying to pull the ball and they give away the outside part of the plate. And if they do get their pitch on the inside part of the plate, there's a chance they'll hook it foul. How many times have you seen a guy pull a ball foul into the upper deck and then strike out on the next pitch?

What the hitters say

HAROLD BAINES I very rarely go up looking to hit a home run because that changes my whole swing. I'm a line drive hitter. I don't have the uppercut swing that most home run hitters have. If I hit a home run it's going to be a line drive. When I hit a home run, it's usually to right-center or left-center. I very rarely pull it down the line.

WADE BOGGS My philosophy is to try to hit from left-center to right-center. That's the biggest part of the park. It's not a philosophy of saying "I'm going to try to hit a home run this time." Instead, I'm saying "I'm going to hit the ball as hard as I can." But when you hit from left center to right center, the fences are from 380 feet to 420 feet, and, most times, line drives don't go for home runs, they go for doubles. That's one reason I'm apt to hit more doubles than home runs.

ANDRE DAWSON There have been times when I've gone to the plate and thought of hitting a home run, but not too often. Sometimes you know a pitcher well enough, and you get a feeling that you're going to hit the ball hard, really drive the ball. There have been situations where I've told teammates I was going to hit the ball out of the ballpark, and it happened. It's just a feeling. You don't do it too often, though, because you'd get over-anxious. There's a fine line between driving the ball and popping it up deep to the outfield or fouling it back, just missing.

CARNEY LANSFORD Very rarely do I go to the plate looking to hit the ball out of the ballpark. When the count is in your favor, you can take a big swing. But it seems like every time I've tried to hit a home run, it's never happened. I try to go up to the plate just thinking about making good, solid contact.

RYNE SANDBERG I go to the plate to hit the ball hard and get on base. The only time I would go up to bat with the idea of hitting a home run is late in the game if we need that to win.

Walt Hriniak has taken up where Charlie Lau left off. Among the many men whose careers have brightened after Hriniak's instruction is Boston's Dwight Evans (above), who became one of the most productive hitters of the 1980s.

CHAPTER 5

Charlie Lau's Ten Absolutes

In their books Ted Williams and Charlie Lau present many of the same ideas about hitting.

Williams has the weight of his own accomplishments behind him. He was a great hitter who worked out his theories and applied them himself, with impressive results.

Lau, on the other hand, was a teacher who studied the styles of the great hitters and blended them into a detailed method. His careful analysis of high-speed, slow-motion films revealed fine points that are not obvious to the naked eye.

In turn Walt Hriniak has developed and refined Lau's method. Like Lau, Hriniak was a catcher. He had only 99 at bats during his major league career, with 25 hits—all singles. Early in his minor league career, he played for a team managed by Lau, and Hriniak became a believer in Lau's method. Since retiring as a player, Hriniak has become an influential hitting instructor, first with the Boston Red Sox and currently with the Chicago White Sox, contributing to the success of such players as Wade Boggs, Carney Lansford, Harold Baines and Dwight Evans. His book, *A Hitting Clinic*, was published in 1988.

The Lau/Hriniak method pays great attention to detail and breaks down the mechanics of hitting in a very clear way that the ordinary hitter can easily understand and apply. This method has proven successful and is very suitable for young players, as Texas Rangers star Harold Baines points out.

"The two guys that taught me are Charlie Lau and Walt Hriniak. Charlie Lau died in 1984, and I didn't get the teaching I wanted after that until 1989, when Walt Hriniak came to the White Sox. He took me from .277 back over the .300 mark. I try to do what they taught me every time I go to the plate. And when I work with young guys, I try to teach them what I learned from Charlie Lau and Walt Hriniak."

This book basically teaches the Lau/Hriniak method, with several of Ted Williams's key points blended in.

To be fair, the Lau and Williams theories are not the only ones—there are other ideas about hitting. There is no one style that is right for everyone. Later on, if you meet a hitting instructor who teaches another method, you can decide at that point which

Walt Hriniak, who has become the foremost instructor of Charlie Lau's method.

causes you to open the rest of your body too soon.

5. **Having your bat in the "launching position" when your front foot touches down.** Your swing doesn't start until your stride is complete.
6. **Making a positive, aggressive move back toward the pitcher.** Step into the ball.
7. **A tension-free swing.** Tension is the batter's number one enemy.
8. **Putting your head down when you swing.** The most important absolute of all—if you lift your head, you don't see the ball.
9. **Using the whole field to hit in.** Don't concentrate on pulling the ball.
10. **Hitting "through" the ball and finishing with your bat high.** Don't cut off your swing—follow through completely.

It's important to understand that the ten absolutes are parts of a whole. Each one is a piece of the puzzle, and they all go together.

A balanced stance (Absolute 1) with good movement (Absolute 2) prepares you for a strong weight shift (Absolute 3). Striding with your front toe closed (Absolute 4) and having the bat in the launching position when your toe touches down (Absolute 5) prevent you from opening your hips too soon and mean you are making a positive, aggressive move back toward the pitcher (Absolute 6). The first six absolutes help produce a tension-free swing (Absolute 7). By keeping your head down (Absolute 8), you won't be overly concerned with pulling the ball and you'll be using the whole field to hit in (Absolute 9). Finally, a tension-free swing will help you follow through completely, hitting through the ball and finishing high (Absolute 10).

The ten absolutes are a model. They represent an ideal of perfection, something to strive for—not even the best hitters can get everything right all the time.

As you work with these absolutes, you will adapt them to your own style, making adjustments along the way. As Charlie Lau says, "Previous training, body type, talent, psychological outlook, and dozens of other factors make each player different. You

approach to follow. For now, you're in good hands with these teachings.

Charlie Lau's approach to the mechanics of hitting is based on what he calls "the ten absolutes." *These are the mechanical techniques you will need to practice in order to develop your ability as a hitter.*

Charlie Lau's Ten Absolutes

1. **A balanced, workable stance.** A balanced stance is the foundation of good hitting.
2. **Rhythm and movement in your stance.** Movement helps reduce tension and gives you a start on shifting your weight.
3. **A good weight shift—from a solid back side, you go forward, to hit against a solid front side.** You have to go back before you stride forward.
4. **Striding with a "closed" front toe.** If you point your toe toward the pitcher when you stride, it

can't take a rigid formula for hitting and make everyone conform exactly."

Similarly, when Ted Williams says that hitting is 50 percent from the neck up, he adds, "The other 50 percent is *hitting according to your style*."

Hall of Famer Tris Speaker, whose 3,514 lifetime base hits is the fifth highest total in history, gave this advice about hitting: "Be natural, it's the most important thing."

Or, as Dusty Baker puts it, "When it comes to hitting, there are standard laws, but there is no standard way."

Remember, *you* have to do the hitting. *You* have to feel comfortable.

This is very important.

We all have our favorite ballplayers, and most of us try to imitate them in one way or another. It's only natural that we should want to be like our heroes.

You have to be careful about this, though. The problem is that sometimes your favorite hitter's

Former Chicago White Sox star Harold Baines, here with the Texas Rangers, is a firm believer in the Charlie Lau/Walt Hriniak hitting method.

A balanced, workable stance is the foundation of good hitting.

You have to get your weight back before you stride forward.

When your toe touches down, your bat is in the launching position. You stride first, then you swing.

Striding with a closed front toe, straight back at the pitcher, keeps your shoulder and hips from opening too soon, and helps you keep your head down.

Your head stays down when you swing, which allows you to follow the ball all the way. You can't hit what you don't see.

Follow through completely and finish with your bat high.

style is not right for you. Major leaguers have been playing baseball for many years and have reached the top of their profession through discipline and hard work. A star player develops his personal style gradually, over the course of time, and whatever that style is, it's right for him.

For example, Will Clark is one of the best hitters in the game today, and many youngsters will be tempted to copy his batting form.

Will uses a closed stance, with his front foot closer to the plate than his back foot. If you try this type of stance and it works for you, fine. But if it doesn't, you'll be making a big mistake if you continue to copy Will's stance simply because you admire him.

Will Clark also has a beautiful, tension-free swing, but if you try to swing exactly the way he does, it could backfire because your own natural, tension-free swing may be quite different from his.

By trying to copy somebody else's stance or swing, you may be creating tension in your own stance and swing and in most cases, you'll be doing yourself more harm than good.

When you look at your favorite players, try to see past their personal styles and think about what

makes them successful. As the Giants hitting coach, Dusty Baker has worked with Will Clark, and in discussing the things that make Clark a great hitter, Baker says, "He has great balance, and he gets extended on almost every swing. But he also has great concentration, and there's something else that never shows—he really studies his opponents."

Those are things that you can do yourself in your own way.

Throughout this book, players talk about their individual preferences and differences. You'll find some ideas which may seem to contradict Charlie Lau's teachings. If you find such an idea that interests you, and you want to try it out, by all means, do so. But remember, if it doesn't work for you, don't continue to use it. Find something else that does work.

It can't be said often enough: *you have to find the style that's right for you.* It takes time, trial and error, and practice.

Before you can practice, however, you must have a definite idea of what you're aiming for. Spend as much time as you need going over Chapters 6-10. Don't be discouraged if you don't follow everything at first. If you're working with a partner, discuss the ideas together.

Begin by practicing your swing without a pitched ball. Try slowing everything down and have your partner check you from beginning to end. When you're sure you know what you're aiming for, go out and start hitting.

And remember, wear a batting helmet at all times.

Will Clark uses a closed stance, with his front foot closer to the plate than his back foot.

CHAPTER 6

A Balanced Stance, with Movement

A balanced stance is the foundation of good hitting.

Think about the foundation of a building. If it's not level, the upper stories won't be level either. It's the same with hitting. If you're not balanced at the beginning, everything else is going to be thrown off—your stride, your swing, your follow-through.

There are as many stances as there are hitters, and some pretty good hitters have used some pretty unorthodox stances. But remember, the chances that someone else's stance will be right for you are very slim, especially if it's an unusual one.

It's far more likely that you'll have success starting with a basic, standard batting stance along the lines described in this chapter. Later on, when you've learned the fundamental mechanics of hitting and are applying them consistently, you may choose to tinker with your stance, just as you may occasionally make small adjustments in your stride or swing.

Most players have one stance, but there are a few who change their stance according to the pitcher and/or the situation. Rod Carew was such a hitter. At this point, your best bet is to find one comfortable stance and stick with it.

Batting stances fall into three types: open, closed, and square.

In an open stance, the batter's front foot is farther away from home plate than his back foot. Rich Gedman uses an exaggerated open stance. This stance can be useful for a hitter who wants to pull the ball, or for one who's getting jammed by the inside fastball.

The open stance has its drawbacks, however. When you assume this stance, you open your body to the pitcher—a dangerous risk, because good hitting technique generally requires not opening your hips too soon. The open stance can also cause you to have problems handling outside pitches.

A closed stance is the opposite. The batter's front foot is closer to the plate than the back one. Will Clark's stance is an example of this type. It can work for a hitter who tends to "step in the bucket"—that is, a righthanded hitter whose stride opens up towards third base, or a lefty who strides toward first. It can also be good for hitters who like to take the outside pitch to the opposite field.

There are a couple of problems with the closed

If your batting stance isn't balanced, your stride, swing, and follow-through will also suffer.

stance, too. First, it makes it difficult to pull the inside fastball. Second, your front shoulder is turned in, which causes your nose to block the vision in your back eye. Try it. Take a closed stance and shut your front eye. See how your vision is limited?

The square or parallel stance is exactly that. Both feet are the same distance away from the plate. If you draw a line from your front toe to your back one, the line will be parallel to the inside edge of home plate. Wade Boggs is a good example of a hitter who uses a square stance.

The square stance keeps the rest of your body in line: your hips, shoulders, and head all line up with your feet, and you can see the ball with both eyes. From a square stance you can pull the ball or hit to the opposite field, whichever the pitch and the game situation require. You don't limit yourself to looking for a certain pitch. In addition, it's easier to stay balanced in a square stance.

How far apart should your feet be? About the width of your shoulders. You may like it a little wider or narrower, but avoid extremes, particularly on the wide end. Spreading your feet too far apart can make it hard to stride and shift your weight.

How far away from the plate should you stand?

There's no set rule. It depends partly on how long your arms are. The one thing you want to avoid at all costs is standing too close to the plate. Crowding the plate is a common tendency, and it causes several problems. First, it prevents you from extending your arms fully when you swing—you're more likely to get jammed. Also, you have less time to react to the pitch because unless you swing early, you're not going to make contact with the fat part of the bat. So don't crowd the plate.

Where in the batter's box should you stand? For the most part, you want to stand medium-deep in the box. If you're facing a pitcher with real heat, you might move back a little to give yourself a split-second longer on the fastball. On the other hand, if the pitcher has a wicked curveball that's breaking down and away from you, or a split-finger pitch that drops sharply, try moving up in the box to catch the ball before it breaks too far.

After you've planted your feet, the next step is extremely important. You've got to get your weight on the balls of your feet. If your weight is on your heels, you're off balance, and you won't be able to move quickly. Watch athletes in various sports—tennis, football, basketball, track and field, etc. You'll notice that they all have their weight on the balls of their feet when they're getting ready to move.

Lau and Hriniak recommend a simple way to ensure getting your weight on the balls of your feet in your batting stance: after you plant your feet, first bend at the waist and then at the knees. This will naturally shift the weight to the balls of your feet.

This may seem like an unimportant detail. It's not. Hriniak emphasizes this when he says, "This is a routine that every hitter should practice again and again. It should be a constant, an absolute."

Finally you have to position your bat. Again this is a personal matter. It's impossible to make a hard-and-fast rule about bat position, but there are some general guidelines to follow.

Remember the "launching position" of the bat in Absolute 5? This is where every good hitter's bat is at the end of the stride. The hands are just behind the back shoulder, and the bat is at a forty-five-degree angle to the ground.

Now if this is where your bat has to be just before

Stan Musial, Jerome Walton, Brian Downing, and Rickey Henderson (clockwise) are examples of hitters who have been successful using an unorthodox stance.

An open stance. The batter's front foot is farther away from the plate than his back foot.

Rich Gedman uses an extreme example of an open stance.

A closed stance. The batter's front foot is closer to the plate than his back foot.

The square or parallel stance. The batter's feet are the same distance from home plate.

you start your swing, the best idea is to get it somewhere close to that when you're in your stance.

Keep your front elbow close—but not pinned—to your body and your back elbow up. Get your hands somewhere around your back shoulder—be careful not to get them too far back. Try to keep the bat angled about forty-five degrees to the ground. Try different positions. There's room to play around and discover where you're most comfortable.

When you find the bat position you like, check to see where your hands are. Have your partner take a good look, too. You want to know where you are so you can get there each time.

Now, go back to the beginning and put it all together in sequence:

1. Plant your feet.
2. Bend at the waist.
3. Bend at the knees.
4. Get your bat in position.

Do it many times over, until you're sure of how it feels. You want to be sure that your stance is constant.

Up until now, as you've been assuming your stance, your energy and attention have been focused within. When you're settled into your stance, your attention starts to shift outward as you begin to get ready for the pitch.

You can help yourself greatly by taking a couple of deep breaths. "One important aspect of relaxation is in your breathing," says Dusty Baker. "Most guys stop breathing, especially in tight situations. Then they get light-headed and start hyperventilating. The next thing you know, they're swinging at anything because they're panicky. Breath deeply and slowly, inhaling through your nose and exhaling through your mouth. That way you get proper oxygen to your brain and your heart, and you can think clearly and concentrate."

Focus your vision on the letter on the pitcher's cap. This will help you a few seconds later, when you look to the pitcher's release point to pick up the ball.

Picture a basketball player, preparing to drive to the basket: waist and knees bent, weight on the balls of the feet, the player's body sways this way and that, getting ready to explode toward the hoop.

A hitter should have some kind of rhythmical movement in his stance while waiting for the pitch. This is one of the ideas which goes against earlier teaching. Batters used to be taught to stay as still as possible in the batter's box, and some batters still practice this.

Today, however, many hitters and hitting instructors have come to believe in movement. This is not to say that you should be jumping all over the place while you wait for the pitch. Some type of gentle, rhythmical movement is what you want.

Imagine a tennis player waiting to receive an opponent's serve: waist and knees bent, weight on the balls of the feet, the player's body is in motion, ready to make a lightning quick move to the ball.

Dusty Baker believes so strongly in movement that he's had speakers installed in the Giants batting cage so the batters can hit to music. "I tell my hitters to have a song in their minds when they're at bat," he says.

Putting some kind of rhythmical movement in your stance helps you in three ways. First it helps you reduce tension and stay relaxed—if you're moving, you're less likely to tighten up your muscles. Second it puts you in motion, which gives you a start on shifting your weight—it's much harder to get going from a still position than a moving one. Third it helps you keep balanced because your weight stays on the balls of your feet.

Like so many aspects of hitting, movement is a matter of individual preference and comfort. Some hitters sway or rock, shifting their weight forward and back several times. Others wiggle their hips slightly. Some batters' movement can be observed in the upper body or the motion of the bat. Some hitters just have an internal rhythm that can hardly be seen.

You have to experiment and see what works for you. Charlie Lau recommends a couple of easy practice swings—after you've planted your feet and bent at your waist and knees—as a way of starting your movement. Keep moving as long as the pitcher is getting ready to wind up. If he takes too long for your satisfaction, step out of the batter's box, compose yourself, step back in, and start over.

Then, just before you start your stride, settle down.

Wade Boggs uses a square stance.

Crowding the plate prevents you from extending your arms and cuts down on your reaction time, so you're more likely to get jammed and less likely to get the sweet spot of the bat on the ball.

Bend at the waist, then at the knees to make sure you get your weight on the balls of your feet.

The launching position is just behind the back shoulder, at a forty-five-degree angle to the ground, so it makes sense to hold your bat somewhere near that position at the start.

Keep your front elbow near your body, your back elbow up, and your hands somewhere around your back armpit.

What the coach says

DUSTY BAKER I think the first thing to talk about in hitting is balance—it starts with your feet and staying on your toes. A lot of guys put too much weight on their heels. You want the weight to be on the balls of your feet.

I believe in movement. You cannot do anything from a dead standstill. All the good hitters I've seen move. You have to have rhythm. The worst thing a hitter can have is tension. When tension sets in, you're in trouble. I've seen guys get so tense, they can't swing. They come back to the bench, and I ask them, "What were you looking for?" and they say, "I was looking for that pitch, but I froze and I just couldn't swing." That's why you move. If you can eliminate the tension, that's half the battle right there.

What the hitters say

HAROLD BAINES I think one of the most important things about hitting is having a well-balanced stance. I try to keep my feet a shoulder width apart and parallel. Aside from that, more than anything else, I concentrate on how far away from the plate I want to stand. I try to get the right distance away from the plate. Because of repetition, if I get that right, everything else falls into place. I try to stand back in the box on lefthanded pitchers. I can see the ball a little bit longer. I wiggle my hips a little bit. It keeps me in a certain rhythm and helps my timing.

WADE BOGGS I've been using my present stance since I was 18 months old. My front foot is right on the front of the plate. It's a guideline I use to stay in the same spot in the box all the time. I don't adjust my stance. A lot of times when you adjust, you create problems. It's hard enough to work with one solid stance.

The main thing about hitting is a law of physics. What is in motion tends to stay in motion. That's really all hitting is. When you're dead in the box—no movement—it creates a lot more energy to get something going than having some movement, some rhythm in the box, and turning it around, shifting your weight back to go forward.

Movement can also be used as an outlet for tension. You can also take a deep breath to relieve tension.

ANDRE DAWSON When I step in, I like to make sure there are no holes and cover up any rough spots. I like to dig into a spot with my back leg. I use a closed stance, with my left leg closer to the plate. My timing mechanism is to wave the bat two, three, four times and get into a set position. If the pitcher hasn't taken a sign by then, if he's taking too long, I'll step out.

I've made adjustments in my stance against certain types of pitchers. I've opened up on occasion when I've face a tough sinkerball pitcher. You see it a little bit sooner than you do from a closed stance.

I think some hitters use movement for a timing mechanism. It depends on the individual. I try to be as still as possible in my stance. I try to keep my concentration focused in on the pitcher, and I'm not going to make a move until I see his hand get ready to come forward. I do wiggle or move my fingers a little bit before the pitcher starts his delivery. One thing you're always taught is to use as light a grip as possible—it helps reduce tension.

CARNEY LANSFORD I have a spot where I like to get in the batter's box. I check to see that I'm the right distance away from the plate—I like to get on the plate a little bit more than a lot of guys. I make sure my feet are the proper width—a little wider than a shoulder's width apart.

I concentrate on not getting too crouched in my stance, because I have a tendency to do that. I don't think about my hands or elbows that much. I just make sure the bat isn't lying on my shoulder. Keep it away and back.

I think you have to have some type of movement to help you stay relaxed. You don't want to be tense when you're hitting.

DON MATTINGLY If I've got a guy that I feel I can handle everything he's got, then I get right on top of the plate. I vary my placement in the box. Closer to the plate and back. With a pitcher who can't throw the ball by me, I don't want to give him the outside corner, so I move up.

EDDIE MURRAY I have about four different stances, and I keep switching off. Usually I'll stand at the back of the batter's box. I may vary, depending on the pitcher.

RYNE SANDBERG I try to do the same thing every time I step into the box. I dig a small hole for my back foot and I like to have a flat front to land, so if there's a hill or a hole up there, I'll flatten that out. That way I know where my feet are going to be. I try and keep my feet even. Sometimes I close my stance a little bit. With certain pitchers, I open up my front leg a little bit to see the ball better. Then I have a few little things I do for rhythm and timing.

I think the movement is the thing that really keeps me ready. Some guys stand real still in the box, and then the ball's coming and they try and do everything at once. I have a slight rock for timing. Then, when I'm ready, I end up back. That's just for me. I think everybody's different, but I think all hitters have some kind of timing mechanism that works for them. I think if you have a little movement, it's relaxing.

Ted Williams coordinated his hips, hands, and front knee in going back, cocking his hips and hands as he moved his front foot to stride.

CHAPTER 7

Weight Shift and Stride

When you throw a ball, you don't just step and throw. First you shift your weight to your back leg so that you can get your momentum going forward.

When you split wood, you don't simply hold the ax over your head and then bring it down. You wind up and bring the ax back, with your weight on your back leg, before you swing the ax up over your head and transfer your weight forward.

When a golfer tees off, there's a backswing first, and at the top of the backswing, the golfer's weight is all on the back leg.

There are dozens more examples of actions which begin with "going back in order to go forward." You might hear this idea expressed as "putting your body into it" or "getting your weight behind it." They all mean the same thing—using your power in the most efficient way.

Hitting is no different. To get maximum power, you have to get your weight back before you start forward. "It's a pendulum action," says Ted Williams. "A metronome—move and countermove. You go back, and then you come forward."

Going back is also a helpful timing mechanism. You start back at the same time the pitcher's arm starts back. That way you are coordinated with him. Working in sync with the pitcher will also help you make a positive, aggressive move back toward him, which is necessary for attacking the ball properly.

When you go back, your weight is transferred onto your back leg. Or, if it makes more sense to you, you might say your weight is "on top" of your back leg. Since your back leg is now supporting your weight, it naturally becomes rigid—it has to, or you would collapse. This doesn't mean your knee is locked—it just means the muscles in your back leg are working to support your weight.

Ted Williams coordinated his hips, hands, and front knee in going back, cocking his hips and hands as he moved his front foot to stride. Williams taught turning the front knee as a cocking mechanism.

Turning the front knee in brings the front heel up off the ground, which in turn causes the hips to rotate back and forces the weight onto the back leg. Wade Boggs uses this technique. Some hitters turn their front shoulder in a bit. Others draw their hands

When you throw a ball, you shift your weight back before you start forward.

back a little. Some simply rock their weight back.

How far back do you want to go? Obviously not so far that you could topple over onto the catcher. Your weight is back, but you're still balanced, even though your balance is now on your back leg. Generally speaking, the farthest you want to go back is to the point where your head is directly over your back leg.

Up until this point, you've been concentrating your vision on the letter on the pitcher's cap. As his arm starts forward, look to his release point and say to yourself, "ball." This will help you focus in and pick up the pitch.

When you get to the place where you're back as far as feels right, you're ready to start your stride. You're still working off the pitcher's motion: just before the ball is released, you begin your stride. Not your swing, but your stride. You *don't step and*

swing at the same time. You step in order to hit. Two distinct actions.

This part is tricky. *You start to stride, but your upper body doesn't follow.* Your upper body has to stay back—this keeps your weight back. If you think of "reaching" with your front leg, instead of "striding," you'll get the idea. Your leg "reaches," but your upper body, and therefore your weight, is still back.

"I tell my hitters to lead with the lower half of the body," says Hriniak in *A Hitting Clinic.* "As the pitcher's arm goes back, the hitter turns his front leg and starts the lower half of his body back. Obviously, the top half will follow. But as the top half moves back, the bottom half will have already been back and essentially have started forward into the stride."

Why is it so important to keep your upper body and your weight back at this point? Because if your weight shifts forward too early, your power is gone.

Once you've started your stride you should be thinking, "front toe closed," and stepping right back at the pitcher.

Striding with a closed front toe means that when your front toe lands, your foot should be as close as possible to the same parallel position as it was in your stance. If you land with your front toe closed, it keeps you on the balls of your feet, it prevents your hips from rotating open too soon, and it keeps your shoulder in and your head down.

On the other hand, if you open up your toe and point it toward the pitcher, you land on your heels, your hips start to rotate, your shoulder follows your hips, and your head comes up.

You might be lucky and catch an inside fastball out in front of the plate, and if you do, you might pull it and give it a nice ride. But if you get any other pitch in any other location, you'll be swinging at air.

So think "front toe closed." Actually your front toe will usually open a bit when you stride. That's all right. The important thing is to keep it from opening too much.

Keep your stride short. If you overstride, you bring your upper body and weight forward too soon, which throws you off balance and costs you power.

The other thing that's essential here is the di-

You start your weight shift back at the same time the pitcher's arm starts back.

Your weight is transferred onto your back leg. You can also think of it as your weight being "on top" of your back leg. At this point your head is over your back leg.

Turning the front knee in forces your hips to rotate back and your weight onto your back leg.

Your weight is still back when your front leg begins the stride. As you start your stride, your hands also start back.

Striding with a closed front toe keeps you on the balls of your feet, and it also keeps your hips closed, your shoulder in, and your head down.

Opening your toe when you stride throws your weight onto your heels and pulls your hip and shoulder open and your head up.

When your front toe touches down, your bat is in the launching position. Your weight is still back.

When your front heel touches down, your weight is distributed evenly onto both legs.

rection of your stride. "To be a good hitter, you have to make a positive, aggressive motion back at the pitcher," says Lau.

"Your stride is pretty much square to the pitcher," says Williams.

It seems so obvious—after all, that's where the ball is coming from. So why would anyone *not* step right back at the pitcher?

One reason is fear of getting hit by the pitch. This is where mental discipline is necessary. Just about everybody who's ever played this game has had to deal with the fear of getting hit. But, surprisingly, your chances of avoiding serious injury are a lot better if you step right back at the pitcher.

You've taken a positive, aggressive stride, with your front toe closed, right back at the pitcher. When that front toe lands, it should land softly. This won't be hard if your weight is still back. Remember, "reach" with that front foot, don't stomp with it. If you stomp, your weight will shift forward too soon. "Reach" aggressively, but land softly. It may sound like a contradiction, but when you do it right, you'll feel it.

When you begin your stride, your hands also start back. Your front leg and your hands work together, so that when your front toe lands, your bat should be in what Charlie Lau calls the "launching position." From his study of slow-motion films and videotapes, Lau noticed that regardless of the differences in stances and bat positions at the start, good hitters all brought their bats to the same place right before the swing: hands just behind the back shoulder, with the bat at about a forty-five-degree angle over the shoulder.

"At this point, if you drop your bat, it should land behind your back foot," says Dusty Baker. "The guys that are in trouble are the ones that bring their hands with them when they stride."

Front toe landed, weight back, bat in the launching position. Ready to swing? Not quite yet. Your front heel has to touch down first, and when it does, it should have the effect of evenly distributing your weight onto both legs.

Remember that we're talking here about fluid motion and incredibly small increments of time. We're attempting to break down the process of weight shift into its parts, but in reality there are not always such clear divisions between the stages. As Dusty Baker says, "The weight shift is the hardest thing about hitting to describe in words. You have to trust your own instincts to a certain degree."

The most important things to understand are (1) you have to go back in order to come forward, (2) your weight is still back when you stride, with a closed front toe, right back at the pitcher, (3) at the moment your front toe touches down softly, your bat is in the launching position, and (4) when your front heel comes down, your weight is evenly distributed onto both legs.

At this point your weight shift is still not finished because you haven't yet transferred your weight completely in order to work against your front leg. That will happen next, as your hips begin to open and you explode into your swing.

What the coach says

DUSTY BAKER You have to have some sort of cocking motion to transfer the weight from the front side back. It's like the hammer on a pistol. Now the pitcher and the hitter are basically doing the same thing, except he has a ball and I have a bat. He goes into his wind-up by going back into a sideways position, exploding toward me, and trying to end up square to me in order to field. I'm starting sideways, going back and trying to end up square to the field. So I time my cocking motion with him—equal and opposite reaction.

What the hitters say

HAROLD BAINES I lift my leg up real high when I stride. It gets me to go back before I go forward. I want to go back to get my weight pretty sturdy so I can have the force to go forward. I try to stride right back at the pitcher.

WADE BOGGS In order to have a good

weight shift, you have to go back to go forward. I call it the pendulum effect. You can't start in an inert state, with your weight balanced fifty-fifty, on the balls of your feet, and then go forward. That's not really weight transfer. You have to go back to go forward. That's what weight transfer is all about.

I try to land in the same spot every time—just to the third base side of the pitcher.

ANDRE DAWSON Just before the pitch is delivered, I do what I call "setting up." I like to take my hands back just a little bit, and in doing so, my hips will rotate likewise.

I try to keep my weight on my back leg and have as short a stride as possible. If I sense my weight is sitting on my back leg, I know I'm going to have a soft stride. You want to soften your stride. If you're facing a pitcher whom you know you can hit hard, you can be too aggressive, and you get yourself out. Over and over, you hear players come back to the bench saying, "I don't know how this guy's getting me out." They're too anxious, too overaggressive.

I try to step at the pitcher. If I step to the left of the mound, I know that my hips will be opening up too soon, my shoulder will fly open, and my head will come off the ball—you can't see the pitch away. If I step too much toward the plate, my hips won't open up—you don't see the inside pitch and you can't turn on it. My toe is opened at a slight angle toward the pitcher's mound.

TONY GWYNN When my front foot lands, I am going toward the pitcher, but my body is going toward the plate. When I am going good, I have a short stride. I start off pretty much balanced, but when I take the stride, when the front leg lands, there is no weight on it.

DON MATTINGLY I need some sort of weight shift to hit the ball with more power. It's simple. I have to go back before I can go forward. It has helped me put the ball in the seats, which I never did before.

EDDIE MURRAY I'm very aggressive. I get in trouble when I overstride.

RYNE SANDBERG I try to stride to the same place, and I like to keep the stride as short as possible. Basically, just pick up the foot and put it down. Six inches is fine. When you stride too far, your whole body is going forward. The shorter the stride, the better you can stay back. A shorter stride also means quicker hands because you can't swing the bat until your foot is down. When I have problems, I tend to overstride, and then I have to correct that. There are times in batting practice where I'll take a round and not stride at all. That helps me to be balanced, stay back, and not overstride.

The ideal thing is to sit back on the back leg and as you stride, just pick up your front foot and still have the balance of staying back.

CHAPTER 8

The Swing: Hips, Hands, and Head

Now you're ready to put the bat on the ball.

In the old days, batters—especially power hitters—were taught to hit off the back leg. It was one of those mistaken ideas that got passed along from one generation to the next, until slow-motion films showed that good hitters—including the great sluggers—had their weight against a rigid front leg at the moment of contact. (In fact, much of the time, good mechanics result in the back leg actually coming up off the ground after contact.)

You've prepared yourself for this by going back to go forward, and by striding, with your front toe closed, right back at the pitcher. Your weight, after your front heel comes down, is evenly distributed onto both legs.

You're at the hitter's moment of truth. What do you do?

You wait. You can't hit the ball until it reaches you. You've made a positive, aggressive move, you're balanced and poised, ready to swing, but if you start your swing too soon, you've given up your advantage. If the pitch is a curveball or a changeup, or if the pitcher takes just a little bit off his fastball, you're going to be out in front.

"Before you start your swing, you have to identify the speed of the pitch," says Dusty Baker.

The idea is to explode on the ball with maximum power. As Ted Williams taught for years, *maximum power comes from the rotation of your hips, which whips your bat around.* Your hips lead your hands.

Try this: stand with your feet apart and your arms hanging limply at your sides. Turn your head in the direction you would be facing if you were batting— to the left if you bat righthanded, to the right if you're a lefthanded hitter. Imagine you're facing a pitcher. Now, with your arms still dangling at your sides, turn your hips toward the imaginary pitcher. See what happens to your arms? Your hips pull them around. That's the way you want it to work in hitting. "The hip movement is a spinning action, with the head as the axis," says Williams.

Remember Absolute 3 in Charlie Lau's model of hitting mechanics: *A good weight shift—from a solid back side, you go forward, to hit against a solid front side.*

Also remember that at the end of your stride, your

weight shift is not yet complete—when your front heel touches down, your weight is evenly distributed onto both legs. Here's the payoff: *it's the exploding open of your hips, at the last possible moment, that completes your weight shift.* When you start to open your hips, your front leg muscles firm up, giving you the solid front side to work against when you swing.

And that's why you have to wait for the ball. If you open your hips too soon, you're ahead of the pitch, and you're uncorking your power too early.

Now you can also see why it was so important to keep your weight back when you began your stride—if you bring your weight forward too soon, you've lost the solid front side to explode against.

Try it. Take a stride and shift your weight onto your front leg as you step. Try to open your hips.

There's nothing to work against. No power. You sacrifice power the same way if you overstride, because overstriding causes you to bring your weight forward too soon.

Your power is in your hips. Yet if you go back and review Charlie Lau's ten absolutes of hitting, you'll notice that he never mentions the hips. It's not that he doesn't recognize the importance of the hips. He does say that "true power in hitting comes from the lower half of your body."

The reason Lau is careful not to emphasize the hips is that many hitters have what we call a "quick hip." In other words, they're so eager to explode on the ball that they open their hips too soon. Lau prefers to have the hitter concentrate on striding with a closed front toe, a proper weight shift, and keeping the head down. He maintains that if those

Stand with your arms at your sides and turn your head in the direction you would to face a pitcher.

Turn your hips toward the pitcher and notice how your arms are pulled around by your hips.

As your hips explode open, your weight shift is complete, as the muscles in your front leg firm up and give you a solid front to swing against.

If you're having trouble getting your hips into your swing, try lifting your back heel and pivoting on your back toe. This will force your hips open.

If you shift your weight forward too soon, you have nothing to work against when you try to open your hips, and your swing will be all arms. No power.

If you open up your hips too early, you lose the power that comes from their opening.

If your weight doesn't shift forward, you'll also be swinging only with your arms.

As your hips open, your hands start forward and down. Your back elbow comes down and in close to your body. Your hips lead your hands, which are out in front of the bat. Your shoulders start to open.

If you start your hands back, it puts a loop in your swing.

Good hitters appear to be attacking the ball with the knob of the bat.

are right, the hips will automatically work correctly.

Whether or not you choose to concentrate on your hips, keep in mind that you cannot generate your maximum power unless your hip action is properly coordinated with your swing. And if you do focus on your hips, remember that you must wait until the last possible instant before you open them up.

There is a mechanical technique which you can use to get your hips working properly without actually concentrating on them. Begin by taking your stride. Get your weight evenly balanced on both legs, as it should be at the end of your stride, when your front heel touches down. Now, lift your back heel and pivot on your back toe, so that your knee points toward the pitcher. This forces your hips open.

If you're having trouble getting your hips into your swing, you can use this technique as a corrective measure. If, because of a bad weight shift, you're either too far out in front or too far back, you'll wind up swinging only with your arms, which means with no power. Waiting for the ball, lifting the back heel, and pivoting on the back toe will help correct this problem.

At the point when your hips start to open, your hands start forward and down, which is the shortest distance to the ball. If you start the other way, you put a loop in your swing, which causes several problems.

First of all, if you loop your swing it takes your bat longer to get to the ball, so you have to commit yourself to swinging sooner—you have less time to decide if it's a pitch you want to hit. Second you don't have as much bat control because your arms are moving away from your body, giving you less leverage against the weight of the bat—the farther away from your body, the heavier the bat gets. Third a loop in your swing throws your weight shift out of whack by redirecting your weight back when it should be moving forward. Finally a looping start is usually followed by an uppercut stroke and such a swing sharply decreases the points of possible contact for the bat and ball as they travel through the hitting zone.

By bringing your hands forward and down, you keep your swing short and compact and reduce the number of things that can go wrong.

You want to bring your bottom hand directly to the ball. It's as if you're trying to attack the ball with the knob of the bat. If you look at photos of all good hitters at this point in the swing, the knob of the bat points directly at the ball.

As your hands move forward and down, your back elbow comes down and in close to your body. Your front shoulder begins to open. Your hips are leading your hands, which are well out in front of the rest of the bat.

One of the trickiest points of hitting is the direction of the swing. Level, up, or down?

The "level swing" used to be one of the main pieces of hitting advice that just about everybody knew. Ted Williams challenged that doctrine in his book, insisting that the best swing was slightly up. His reasoning was that since the pitcher is standing on a hill and releasing the ball at the top of his reach, the ball is coming toward you at a downward angle. Therefore, in order to have the greatest chance of hitting the ball, the batter needs to swing slightly upward.

What Williams says makes sense. In fact, if you're going to follow through properly, it's necessary to swing slightly upward in order to finish with your bat high (Absolute 10).

The danger in the slightly upward swing is falling into the big uppercut stroke that so many home run hitters use. The uppercut swing goes with the loop we described earlier and puts you at a big disadvantage.

Charlie Lau and Walt Hriniak like the level swing, though both agree that the slightly upward swing is acceptable. Lau actually advocates a downward swing, particularly as a remedy against the uppercut: " . . . a slight uppercut, . . . as long as it remains slight, isn't all that bad. In fact, it's possible that in the perfect swing you do have a slight uppercut. The problems occur when the uppercut is an extreme loop. That's what you want to stay away from, and getting on top of the ball by swinging down is usually a good way to counteract this tendency. Ideally, the two motions will cancel each other out, and result in a *level* swing."

Ted Williams says something similar: "The level

swing . . . is the shortest possible stroke; you have less chance of hitching, of overswinging. It helps you get back on top of the ball and, more important, gives you more time to wait, to keep from getting fooled."

When you chart the ideal swing from beginning to end, it's actually U-shaped. It starts down, turns slightly upward just before meeting the ball, and continues up into the follow-through. The outline of the U will vary, depending on where the ball is—on a pitch higher in the strike zone, the swing will be a flatter U than the swing on a low pitch.

The hitting zone—where you make contact with the ball—is roughly from the back of the plate to two feet out in front of the plate. You want your bat to be coming through that zone on the same plane as the flight of the ball for as much of your swing as possible. The swing that maximizes that time is the U-shaped swing.

This is why the looping, uppercut swing decreases your chances for making contact. An uppercut swing takes your bat's trip through the hitting zone away from the plane of the ball's flight—the more severe the uppercut, the less time your bat is co-ordinated with the ball's flight, and therefore you have fewer points where you can make contact.

One of the most mistaken ideas ever taught about hitting, is that you roll your top hand over as you meet the ball. Where this notion of "rolling the wrists" got started is not clear, but it used to be one of the most accepted, basic ideas of all.

But if you look at pictures of good hitters at the moment of contact, the palm of the bottom hand is always facing down and the palm of the top hand is always facing up. *Always.*

Williams compares it to swinging an ax at a tree. When you chop down a tree with an ax, you wouldn't dream of rolling your wrists as you hit the

Good hitters always have the palm of the top hand facing up and the palm of the bottom hand facing down at the moment of contact.

Your wrists do not roll until well after the moment of contact.

trunk of the tree. And you shouldn't hit a baseball that way—not if you want any power. As Williams says, "You get your power not so much from the wrists or the arms and shoulders, but from the rotation of the hips into the ball."

Your wrists do not roll over until later in the follow-through, well after the ball has left the bat.

The last element in your swing, and in many ways the most important of all, is your head. Charlie Lau says, "If I could tell . . . young players only one thing that would improve their hitting, it would be this: *Your head goes down when you swing* . . . good hitters see the ball longer than poor hitters. Your

Your head stays down when you swing, and you follow the ball all the way with your eyes.

mechanics can be good, and your swing can be good. But if you don't see the ball, you're not going to hit it. Even if the rest of your mechanics are rotten, if your head goes down when you swing, you can still have a degree of success."

What Lau is talking about here is following the ball all the way with your eyes. It's a more precise and clearer way of stating the old cliche "keep your eye on the ball," which, while good advice, doesn't tell you anything about *how* to do it.

Part of how to do it is mechanics. If your front foot opens toward the pitcher when you stride, it will pull your front hip, shoulder, and head open, and you'll have trouble keeping your eye on the ball. Or if you have a quick hip, you'll also have trouble keeping your eye on the ball because your head will come up. But even if you've done all the other things correctly, you still have to discipline yourself to keep your head down, following the ball.

How far does your head go down? Not very far. We're not talking about taking a bow. Really, the ideal is probably to keep your head basically still, but that is very difficult to achieve. Instead, if you concentrate on following the ball with your eyes, all the way from the pitcher's point of release to the point of contact with your bat, your head will take care of itself.

Actually, if you watch many good hitters, you'll see that when they take a pitch, they watch the ball all the way into the catcher's mitt. Wade Boggs is a master at this.

To review the key elements of the swing: (1) wait for the ball, (2) explode your hips open at the last moment, (3) start your hands forward and down, (4) swing level or slightly upward just before contact, (5) at the moment of contact, the palm of the bottom hand faces down and the palm of the top hand faces up, and (6) your head goes down as it follows the ball all the way from the pitcher's release point to the point of contact with your bat.

Andre Dawson of the Chicago Cubs knows how important it is to "keep your head in," even after the follow-through, no matter how hard you swing.

What the coach says

DUSTY BAKER Attack the ball with the knob of your bat. If you lead with the knob, you are going directly to the ball. No matter where the ball is, lead with the knob and keep your hands above the ball. You want to start your swing short and finish long.

If you stay on the plane of the ball, with a flat swing or a slight uppercut, you have a much better chance of hitting the ball.

Your hips lead your hands through the zone, not the other way around. Your power comes from your legs.

Your eyes are the most important thing about hitting. You can't hit what you don't see. When you put your head down on contact, it's like shooting a rifle. You sight down the barrel of your bat just like sighting down the barrel of a rifle. It keeps you on target. Also, when you put your head down, you activate the muscles in your back and neck, which gives you extra strength.

What the hitters say

HAROLD BAINES I was taught that your head controls everything because if you don't see the ball, it doesn't matter how good your hands are. If I keep my head straight, I'm going to see the ball on the same plane. If I keep my head straight and watch the ball all the way to the plate, I have a better chance of making contact.

My head should be fairly straight, on the ball. I don't want to watch the ball to see where it goes. I try to see the ball hit the bat, and even after, leave my head right there. It keeps me in the right frame of mind for seeing the ball all the time. A lot of times your tendency is to pull your head off at the point of contact. That gets you in the rut of not seeing the ball as long as possible. I'm speaking for me—I don't know about anybody else.

WADE BOGGS I don't really concentrate on my hips at all. They stay true as long as my head is on the ball. If you stay on the ball, your hips should work right.

You start your swing down because you want to keep your bat head above the ball. But when you get into the impact zone, you have to swing slightly up to meet the arc of the ball. It's coming from a higher plane. It's just common sense that you're going to have a greater impact when the ball's traveling on a downward plane if the bat's traveling on an upward plane than you would with the bat traveling on a level plane. You're going to have a lot greater impact zone. Your contact area will be a lot greater.

Your head is the key to hitting. You have to see what you're hitting. Striding with a closed toe enables you to keep your head in there a little longer.

ANDRE DAWSON I think your hips are the finish of your swing. They help you get through the ball. When I watch films of guys with good mechanics and good bat speed, the hips seem to be the last thing to come into play.

I don't like to move my head. When you move your head, the ball moves, too. Sometimes I'll rest my head on my left shoulder, and as soon as I start my swing it will come off. I like to see the ball hit my bat. It's not going to happen every at bat during the season, but I try to remain conscious of that and come close to it.

DWIGHT EVANS Put your head where you hit the ball. A lot of great hitters do it without even realizing it.

CARNEY LANSFORD You don't want to open up your hips too soon, but once you do, you use them to guide the ball. If you open too soon, you'll fly out. Keeping your head down on the ball is the most important thing. You can have the best swing in the world, but if you don't watch the ball, it doesn't do you any good.

I don't swing up. If anything, I try to swing a little down. You think you're swinging down, but you're actually swinging level. I practice swinging down a little bit when I'm in the on-deck circle. I'm more of a line drive hitter, and if I hit the ball in the air, there's a chance it'll be an out.

EDDIE MURRAY I try to meet the ball when it's right in front of me. If I'm a little late and hit it even with me or a little behind me, I just won't hit it well.

RYNE SANDBERG My hips are where all my power is. It's just a natural thing for me. It's noth-ing I really work on. If you're doing your stride right, and if your hands and legs are correct, I think your hips come naturally. I think it would be hard to go up there and say, "I'm going to think about my hips this at bat." If you do the other things correctly, your hips should work automatically.

Your head stays still. You don't want a whole lot of movement forward or across the plate with your head. Just a nice, still head, watching the ball all the way to the plate—even all the way to the catcher's glove. That's the number one thing about hitting.

CHAPTER 9

Hitting to All Fields

"Everybody's trying to *pull* the ball . . . Almost everybody, from the left fielder to the utility shortstop, is trying to hit home runs, which is folly . . . ," says Ted Williams.

The surprising thing about hearing this from Williams is that he was one of baseball's all-time great power/pull-hitters. Batting lefthanded, Williams was so skilled at hitting to right field that the Cleveland Indians used a shift against him in which the shortstop and third baseman moved over to the right side of second base, the second baseman played a short right field, and the left fielder was positioned in short left-center.

In spite of the fact that this shift opened up the entire left side of the field, Williams still kept hitting to right. "Everybody was saying . . . that I wasn't trying to hit to left, that I was too stubborn, that all I cared about was ramming the ball into the teeth of that shift, getting base hits in spite of it," he explains. "The fact was, I was having a hard time learning to hit to left."

Eventually he did learn to hit the opposite way, and the shift became less effective.

The most consistent batters are the ones who can hit the ball to all parts of the field. And keep in mind that you can hit the ball just as hard up the middle and to the opposite field as you can when you pull it.

Of course there are situations and pitches which call for pulling. Pulling the ball is part of hitting to all fields. But you should be smart and selective about when you try to pull.

The most obvious component in hitting to all fields is where the ball is pitched. It's clearly easier to pull the inside pitch, go up the middle with the pitch down the heart of the plate, and drive the outside pitch to the opposite field.

But there's more to it than that. Another factor in where the ball goes is *when* you make contact: at the beginning of your swing—that is, in the back of the hitting zone—the ball tends to go to the opposite field; in the middle of your swing it tends toward center field; at the end of your swing—in the front of the hitting zone—you're more likely to pull the ball.

Another way to control where you hit the ball is

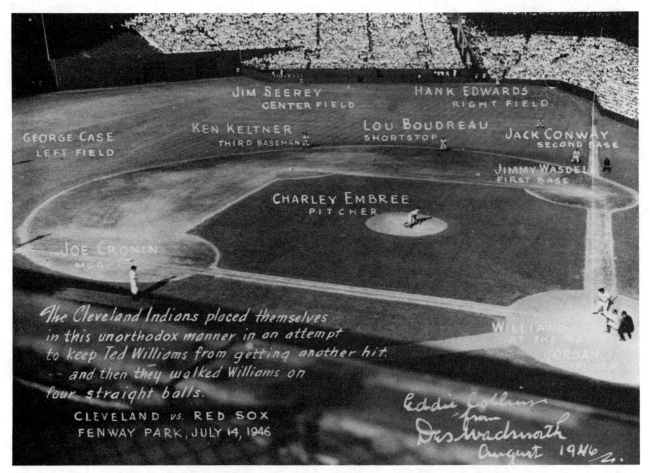

The shift used by the Cleveland Indians against the lefthanded pull hitting of Ted Williams.

where you stand in the batter's box. If you're up in the box and off the plate, you'll tend to hit to the opposite field. If you move back in the box and close to the plate, you increase your chances of pulling the ball.

So if you're in a situation where you want to hit the ball to the opposite field, you can accomplish this in three ways. First, choose an outside pitch. Second, wait a little longer on the pitch down the middle or on the inside part of the plate in order to make contact earlier in your swing. Third, when you take your stance, move up in the box and off the plate.

Charlie Lau advises to try and hit every ball back at the pitcher. The ideal swing on a pitch down the middle of the plate will result in a line drive over second base. This is to say that the bat meets the ball at a ninety-degree angle to its flight path. Unless the ball is hit directly at the pitcher's chest or at the center fielder, it's going to be a base hit.

Unfortunately not every pitch is down the middle of the plate, and even on the ones that are, your

timing has to be perfect to hit it right back up the middle. If your intent is to hit the ball back up the middle, however, your chances of success are much greater than if you're always trying to pull the ball.

Another reason why it's so important to develop a swing that keeps your bat with the plane of the ball's flight as it moves through the hitting zone is that if your timing is just a little bit off and you're early or late, you can still hit the ball hard.

A good rule of thumb is to go with Charlie Lau's advice: (1) concentrate on mechanics and (2) try to hit a line drive to center field on every swing. If you nail the ball, it's a base hit up the middle. If you're a little early, you'll pull it, and if you're a little late, you'll drive it to the opposite field.

So unless you're trying to hit the ball to a certain part of the field in a particular situation, you don't really have to worry about hitting to all fields. As Dusty Baker says, "Just hit the ball hard, and let it go where it wants to."

It's easier to pull the inside pitch, go up the middle with the ball down the heart of the plate, and go the opposite way with the outside pitch.

If you make contact at the beginning of your swing—at the back of the hitting zone—you'll usually hit the ball towards the opposite field. If you make contact in the middle of your swing, it'll normally go up the middle. Contact at the end of your swing results in a pulled ball.

If you move up in the box and off the plate, you increase your chances of hitting to the opposite field. If you move back and closer to the plate, you can pull the ball more effectively.

What the hitters say

HAROLD BAINES My main objective is to hit the ball where it's pitched.

WADE BOGGS I just try to see the ball and hit it where it's pitched. My philosophy of hitting from left-center to right-center helps me stay on the ball a little longer.

ANDRE DAWSON If the pitchers are staying away from you, you need to think of hitting the ball up the middle or hit the ball to the opposite field. If you think that way, you get out of the habit of trying to pull that pitch and get yourself out. And if your swing is right, the ball can go just as far hitting it the other way. If a guy's pitching me that way, I like to think, "Stay behind the ball." You're not really swinging late—you're staying behind the ball and driving it where it's being pitched.

RYNE SANDBERG Hitting the ball to the opposite field is the hardest stroke to have. It takes a lot of discipline. You have to wait on the ball. You can cover the outside pitches and breaking balls away if you can hit the other way. A person has to learn to pull the ball too, but I think pulling the ball comes a little more naturally. In the major leagues I had problems with hard throwers inside and good sinkerballers inside because in the minor leagues and my first couple of years in the big leagues, I was a gap hitter to right center field. It wasn't until 1984 that I learned to turn on the inside pitch in certain situations. I think it's very important to use the whole field when hitting.

CHAPTER 10

Following Through

If you threw a ball and your arm stopped just as you let go of it, how far do you think it would travel? Not very far. To get the maximum velocity and distance on a throw, your arm must follow through after you release the ball—that is, your arm must continue the motion to its completion.

It's the same with hitting. If you stop your swing after you make contact, the ball is not going to carry. To send the ball the greatest possible distance, you must continue your swing after your bat meets it. Charlie Lau calls this "hitting through the ball."

When the ball hits your bat, the force of it will act against the force of your swing. It tends to slow your bat down and check its momentum. You can't let that happen, or your follow-through will suffer.

"When you hit, you've got to extend your arms completely," says Lau. "If you quit at the point of contact, the ball won't go anywhere. And if you don't drive the ball, if you don't follow through, everything you've done up to that point will be wasted."

Lau's technique for executing a full and powerful follow-through is to finish your swing with your bat high. Remember the U-shaped swing? It finishes high.

Just after contact your arms should be fully extended. To maximize the power of your swing, you will want to keep this extension into your follow-through. The reason for finishing high is that it helps you maintain your extension.

This also illustrates why you don't want to roll your wrists at the moment of contact. If you roll your top hand over too soon, you're more likely to finish low and restrict the extension of your arms because your lower arm will be pulled back by your top wrist.

In fact, Lau and Hriniak recommend that at the point in your follow-through where your top hand would begin to restrict the extension of your arms, remove it from the bat. Again it was the study of films which made Lau aware that many great hitters release their top hand toward the end of the swing.

This is one of the most controversial and misunderstood points of the Lau/Hriniak method.

To really understand what Lau and Hriniak are saying, keep two things in mind. First neither insists that every hitter needs to adopt this technique — if you can get full extension in your follow-through and finish high without taking the top hand off, you may not need to do so. Second, if you do release your top hand, it's very important not to do it too soon. One of the biggest misunderstandings of the Lau/Hriniak method is that they teach releasing your top hand just after contact. Not true. Your top hand doesn't come off the bat until the point at which it would begin to restrict the extension of your arms—in other words, when your swing is about three-quarters finished. Releasing your hand any earlier doesn't make sense—you'd be hitting one-handed.

You have to decide for yourself whether you want to remove your top hand or not. Keep in mind that it's still a new idea to a lot of people, so you may get some flak about it. If you want to try it, go ahead. If you feel comfortable with it and it works for you, keep it. If not, don't. Do what's best for you. One more thing about finishing high: it helps you keep your head down. Your chin, which began on your front shoulder, should wind up on your back shoulder. After the ball has left the bat, your head is still down. Resist the temptation to look up after the ball because the longer you can keep your head down, the stronger your follow-through will be. Besides, as Walt Hriniak says, " . . . you don't need to see where the ball goes to start running to first base."

When you throw a ball, your arm follows through after you release it.

The U-shaped swing finishes high.

Just after the moment of contact, your arms are fully extended.

If your top hand rolls over too soon in your swing, it restricts your extension by pulling your lower arm back.

At the point in your follow-through where your top hand begins to limit the extension of your arms, remove it from the bat. This is usually about three-quarters through your swing.

Many great hitters release their top hand toward the end of their swing.

What the coach says

DUSTY BAKER I like taking the top hand off when you have a guy who doesn't stay on the ball through the hitting zone. Or a guy who tries to pull the outside pitch. It applies to certain hitters. But on the inside pitch, I'd rather see two hands on the bat in the follow-through.

Remember: You want to start your swing short and finish long—in other words, extension.

What the hitters say

HAROLD BAINES My release of the top hand came from Charlie Lau. If my top hand stays on, it becomes too dominant, and it has a tendency to pull me off the ball. My front shoulder flies out. The top hand comes off when you think it should come off. Some people think you're swinging with one hand, but that's not true.

WADE BOGGS The upward direction of your bat in the impact zone continues as you finish your swing.

CARNEY LANSFORD I use the Charlie Lau/ Walt Hriniak theory—let the top hand come off the bat once you've had a full swing. Don't let it come off too soon. I'm a big believer in it. A lot of kids do it naturally.

Your chin begins on your front shoulder and winds up on your back shoulder. Your head is still down.

Putting it all together—righthanded

The swing begins with a comfortable, balanced stance in anticipation of the pitch.

As the pitch is delivered, the left foot elevates and steps forward as the weight is shifted back to the right leg.

As the right toe touches down, the hips begin to open, bringing the shoulders and arms around.

Just before contact, it appears that the batter is attacking the ball with the knob of his bat.

When contact is made, the hips are fully opened, weight is evenly balanced, and the right palm is facing up while the left palm is facing downward.

On the follow-through, the batter's arms become fully extended before the hitter rolls his wrists, with the right wrist rolling over the left.

Putting it all together—lefthanded

The swing begins with a comfortable, balanced stance in anticipation of the pitch.

As the pitch is delivered, the right foot elevates and steps forward as the weight is shifted back to the left leg.

As the left toe touches down, the hips begin to open, bringing the shoulders and arms around.

Just before contact, it appears that the batter is attacking the ball with the knob of his bat.

When contact is made, the hips are fully opened, weight is evenly balanced, and the left palm is facing up while the right palm is facing downward.

On the follow-through, the batter's arms become fully extended before the hitter rolls his wrists, with the left wrist rolling over the right.

CHAPTER 11

The Mental Game

As Ted Williams said, "Hitting is 50 percent from the neck up." The mental aspects of hitting are every bit as important as the physical mechanics.

Number one in the mental department is concentration. You have to pay close attention to the pitcher if you expect to gain the advantage. When you're sitting on the bench or waiting in the on-deck circle, watch the pitcher and learn as much as you can in preparation for your turn at bat.

Where is his release point? What is his repertoire of pitches? Does he have a pattern to his pitches? Does he change his delivery on different pitches? Does he always go to one certain pitch when he needs a strike? All these factors play a part in your study of a pitcher.

Another key is pitch selection—knowing what to swing at. Ted Williams's first rule of hitting is to get a good pitch to hit.

The most obvious thing about pitch selection is to lay off pitches that are out of the strike zone. Williams calculated that if you swing at balls just two inches out of the strike zone, you've increased the pitcher's advantage by more than one-third. He emphasized the importance of learning your strike zone, because a hitter who is known to chase bad pitches will be fed a steady diet of them.

Even within the strike zone, there are pitches that you don't want to swing at unless you have two strikes, because the percentages are against your hitting them well. Williams devised a chart showing his success rate with balls in every location of the strike zone. He recommends that all batters make such a chart for themselves based on which locations they handle well and which they don't. Even the best hitters have areas of the strike zone in which they have a greater degree of success, and if you start going out of your area too much, you're increasing the pitcher's chances of getting you out.

As a hitter, you must make the pitcher throw the ball where you want it by refusing to chase the pitches you don't handle well. This takes discipline and patience, but it pays off because most pitchers don't have such pinpoint control that they can repeatedly put the ball in an exact spot. If you can be patient, you will force the pitcher to make a mistake—not every time, but often enough. A batter lives off the mistakes of pitchers.

Another part of the mental game is dealing with fear. All batters experience fear at some time in some form. Besides the fear of failure, there is the fear of getting hit by the pitched ball.

You have to be ready to hit every pitch, so you must make a positive, aggressive move back at the pitcher. But when a young, inexperienced hitter sees a tight pitch, the tendency is to straighten up and bend backward, away from the ball. As Charlie Lau says, "It feels safer to him than being bent forward, but it's the wrong thing to do."

If you straighten up and bend back you're caught flat-footed, off-balance, and your maneuverability decreases. There's only one way to avoid the pitch—

going down backwards—but with limited maneuverability, you're in danger of not being able to move fast enough. Besides, if it's a good slider or curve ball and it breaks over the plate at the last instant, you aren't in any position to swing.

The best technique for avoiding a close pitch is called "rolling." If you're balanced as you stride, and the pitch is too close, you turn or "roll" your front shoulder in toward the catcher. That way if you do get hit by the pitch, at least it won't be in the head or chest. When you practice rolling, use tennis balls at first—they don't hurt.

One of the biggest factors in the mental game is confidence. Believing in yourself is half the battle, and there's nothing like success to build confidence.

Inexperienced hitters tend to straighten up and back away from a tight pitch. This leaves you vulnerable because you are off-balance and the only way you can avoid the pitch is to fall backward. This limits your maneuverability.

The correct way to deal with a tight pitch is to turn your front shoulder in to the catcher. That way you protect your head and chest.

Discipline, practice, homework, and concentration all contribute to building your confidence through success.

Finally one other thing you need to learn about the mental part of hitting is to gain control of your emotions. Baseball is a game where emotional composure is essential. Dusty Baker puts it beautifully when he says, "If you want to be a good hitter, you have to have a burning desire to succeed in your heart, but you must have the coolness of mind in order to control that burning desire."

What the coach says

DUSTY BAKER I believe in watching the pitcher very carefully. Watch his mannerisms, study his tendencies, time his delivery. If you can eliminate giving away at bats through mind lapses, you can be a good hitter. If you go up to the plate unprepared mentally, without doing your homework, you're giving away an at bat. One pitch can change a whole at bat. A checked swing on a high fastball, and you're 1 and 1 instead of 0 and 2. Now you're more in control. If you had swung, you'd only have one chance left. That's that one pitch. If you're not concentrating, you've given away that at bat.

In a tight situation, don't get caught up in the tempo of the game. Step back, breathe, relax, concentrate, and see yourself coming through before it happens. Imagine your success in your mind.

Some batters concede the outside part of the plate to the pitcher, but I don't think any of it should be his. My thinking is, why should he have any of it when he's standing on top of a hill throwing down at me, he's got a catcher working with him against me, and he has seven players behind him to catch the ball? And he wants part of the plate? My idea is don't give him any of it. Okay, there is a part of the plate that I'm not going to make my living off—the low, outside pitch. That's a low percentage pitch to hit. Especially early in the count. I don't want to hit that pitch until I have to.

What the hitters say

HAROLD BAINES I start on the bench, before I even get up to the plate. I try to pick up the pitcher's pattern. In the on-deck circle, I concentrate on picking up the pitcher's release point, and I think about what I want to do before I hit.

WADE BOGGS The mental part of hitting has to do with desire—the drive to be the best. The other part is concentration. Those are the keys.

When I'm on the bench, I watch the pitcher at all times. Same in the on-deck circle. When I study a new pitcher, I look for his velocity, what pitches he throws, if he tips a pitch. Any little telltale sign.

Basically, all concentration is, is thinking of nothing. When you get into the batter's box, you don't want to be thinking of anything. A lot of kids in high school and college—even professionals—when they get in the batter's box, they're thinking about too many different things, and you can run into problems there. When you get into the batter's box, the main thing is to concentrate on the ball.

I consider the most important things in hitting to be patience, concentration, and discipline. You can do everything right mechanically—some guys have the prettiest swing in the world, but they have poor concentration, poor discipline, and poor pitch selection. They're doing everything right mechanically, but they're still hitting .212. If you start out with learning to concentrate, not to go for bad pitches, and to be patient enough to wait for the good pitches, the mechanics can also be learned.

ANDRE DAWSON It takes a lot of work to become a good hitter, and a good portion of it is mental. There's a mental battle between the hitter and the pitcher and catcher. You have to try and outthink the opposition. Most pitchers pitch in a pattern, and until you adjust, that's the way you're going to be pitched.

When I'm on the bench, or in the on-deck circle, I try to zero in on the pitcher and see what kind of stuff he has that day. What's his best pitch? What pitch is he having trouble getting over the plate? How well is he throwing the ball? If it's my first at bat, I'm usually thinking of how this pitcher got me out the last time I faced him.

When you face a new pitcher, you try to look for flaws in his delivery—something that may tip off a certain pitch.

TONY GWYNN If you are in the on-deck circle, watch how the guy pitches the guy at the plate. Just be more knowledgeable, try to learn whatever you can. The bottom line is, if he makes the right pitch, he is going to get me out. If he makes a mistake, I have a chance.

KEITH HERNANDEZ The pitcher has to make a great pitch to me to get it in there every time, and sooner or later he'll make a mistake. It'll be out there and I'll get him. It's a matter of being patient. If he starts me out with a nasty pitch, I'm not afraid to let it go by. I've still got two more swings.

CARNEY LANSFORD Hitting is about 90 percent mental. You have to go to the plate with a positive attitude.

On the bench and in the on-deck circle, I try to concentrate on picking up the pitches. First off, you have to know what kind of pitch selection the pitcher has. I want to know, before I walk into the batter's box, what pitches he has. Also, I try to pick up a pattern he may be throw-

ing to different hitters, especially someone who is a similar kind of hitter to myself.

DON MATTINGLY Each time I go up, I want to get a good pitch to hit and hit it hard. A lot of guys give away at bats. They make a mental mistake here, a mental mistake there.

EDDIE MURRAY You just can't swing at bad pitches. The more you cut down on this, the more the odds come over to your side.

RYNE SANDBERG Preparation starts in the clubhouse before you ever take the field—who's pitching that day, what his pitches are, what his "out" pitch might be, what to look for in certain situations. Most batters, when they step into the box, try to have some idea how the pitcher is going to pitch them. I'm a number two hitter, so I always study how the pitcher pitches the leadoff hitter. I like to see what the guy's fastball and breaking ball are like. It's important for the lead-off hitter to make the guy throw as many pitches as he can, so the following hitters can see what he's throwing. Pitchers change. One time he might not have the same fastball as another time. I like to observe these things from the bench and the on-deck circle. I like to swing a weighted bat in the on-deck circle to get loose and get any kinks out. Get loose, observe, and start concentrating before you get up there. When you step into the box, you don't have time for much else besides hitting.

GARRY TEMPLETON If you can concentrate, hitting is easy. If a person could gear his concentration in, he should be able to hit the ball every time he comes up to the plate.

CHAPTER 12

Slumps

One area where mental discipline can be critical is in dealing with slumps. Everybody has slumps. They're part of the game. The question is how to deal with them.

The worst thing about a slump is that it tends to feed on itself. If you have a bad day at the plate, it's only natural to want to make up for it the next time out. So you try a little harder. You start getting a little tense, looking for a base hit. If it doesn't come in your first two turns, you're maybe zero for your last six at bats. Now you start to lose your confidence, and you begin to wonder if you'll ever get on base again. You get anxious, impatient, start swinging at bad pitches. The tension increases. You're on a downhill mental slide, and unless you turn that negative attitude around, the hole you're in is going to get deeper and deeper.

What can you do?

The worst things you can do are (1) listen to all the advice that everybody is sure to start giving you, and (2) start changing everything and anything in your batting style. When Dwight Evans was in the worst slump of his career in 1980, he tried changing his stance constantly. "I was always trying something different. I'd have a stance for a week, and then I'd have a stance for another week. Open, closed, down low, stand up straight. I was known as The Man of a Thousand Stances." He got on track when he began working with Walt Hriniak.

Often there is one little key change you can make which will help you out of the hole. In 1989 New York Yankees outfielder Jesse Barfield used videotape to analyze his problem. "I watched the tape and I saw what I was doing different," says Barfield. "I had my bat wrapped around my head, and that made for a longer swing."

In 1988 St. Louis Cardinals catcher Tony Pena took a suggestion from manager Whitey Herzog and made an adjustment in his stance, going from a closed stance to more of a square stance. After making the change, Pena went 19 for his next 49 at bats, a .388 batting clip. "Since I opened up my stance, I'm quicker," he says. "My bat probably has 75 percent more speed. I was really slow on the inside pitch. They can pitch me inside now, and I don't even worry about it."

For Ryne Sandberg, the best way to break a slump is to "go back to basics."

If you're struggling at the plate, go back to basics. Concentrate on mechanics, most particularly on keeping your head down, because in almost every case, a hitter in a slump is not seeing the ball. It could be a quick hip, or overstriding, or opening your toe when you stride, or some other factor that's causing you to prematurely come off the ball with your head.

When you're hitting well, you're seeing the ball well. You're picking it up as it leaves the pitcher's hand, and you're getting a good look at it as it approaches the plate. Every batter on a hot streak will tell you that he's seeing the ball well, or that the ball looks as big as a grapefruit.

When you're in a slump, though, the ball will often look like a blur. You might not be picking it up until it's halfway to the plate, and before you know it, it's a fastball that's by you or you're swinging at a curveball in the dirt.

If you concentrate on keeping your head down, you will certainly improve your chances of making contact. Forget entirely about trying to pull the ball. In order to pull you have to open up sooner, and if you're not seeing the ball, that's the last thing you want to do. Instead, wait a little longer and try to hit the ball up the middle, back at the pitcher.

If you can concentrate on keeping your head down, you'll start seeing the ball better, and if you're seeing the ball, you'll start making better contact. If you start hitting the ball harder, the hits will come. Your mental state will begin to change. Your con-

Former St. Louis Cardinals catcher Tony Pena changed his stance, going from a closed stance to a square stance in 1988; he promptly batted .388 in his next 49 at bats.

fidence will return, and you won't be as tense.

Remember also that if you're hitting the ball hard but right at somebody, it's not really a slump—it's just bad luck. Don't change anything.

What the coach says

DUSTY BAKER The better hitters are the ones that can simplify when something's off. It's usually something simple that turns into something complicated and you end up lost. Everybody's telling you what to do, and you're watching films. Most slumps are because of a quick hip.

What the hitters say

HAROLD BAINES For me, a slump is 0 for 10. But if you're hitting the ball hard, 0 for 10 is not a slump. It's bad breaks. If you're hitting ground balls or striking out, that's a slump. When you're hitting well, everything is natural. When you get into a slump, you figure everything's off. You try to change the whole stance, but really you don't have to. It could be something small that you think is major. Or you could be trying to do more than what you really can. Maybe you're swinging a little bit too hard, and that might pull your front shoulder out. That's why it's great to have a video camera. You can go back and review.

WADE BOGGS To me a slump is not getting any hits. I can go 1 for 32 and still hit the ball hard twenty-eight times. For other people a slump is mechanical or mental. To me a slump is just a run of bad luck. You just have to maintain your same swing.

ANDRE DAWSON I think a slump is any time you go about fifteen times at bat without a hit, and you find that you're not hitting the ball on the fat part of the bat. You're not driving the ball. You can be hitting the ball hard and have tough luck and be hitting it right at someone. But when pitchers are getting you out with pitches you should be hitting, somewhere along the line, you have to make a correction in your mechanics. Get back to basics.

A lot of players, when they're in a slump, will make the mistake of starting to experiment, of starting to look for a lot of advice about what they're doing wrong. If you start listening to a lot of outside advice, you can find yourself getting into an even worse rut. In the end, it all boils down to basics and fundamentals. I try to hit the ball to right field, hit back up the middle. I try to wait on the ball, use my hands a little more. If I try to muscle the ball and use my body more, I have a tendency to attack the ball and jump at it. The more you do that, the longer your stride. So I cut down on my stride in batting practice, and try to let that carry over into the game. I think "hit the ball back up the middle." The one thing you don't want to do is be overaggressive. Don't fall into the trap of the pitcher and catcher by swinging at everything that's being thrown.

CARNEY LANSFORD A slump is when you're not hitting the ball hard consistently. If you go through a period when you're hitting the ball hard, that's all you can do—just keep hitting the ball hard. In fact, about the only thing you can do for a slump is keep hitting. I don't think you can go up there and try to do anything different. If you can get away from the mental part, that's a factor, because every time you go to the plate you take a negative aspect up there with you. Try to turn it positive.

DAVE PARKER Usually, when you're in a slump, there's one little thing that puts you back on track.

RYNE SANDBERG A slump is when you're not making good contact with the ball. I go back to my basics. Check my mechanics—stride, hands. I go into batting practice and try to hit the balls up the middle. The problems I have during the season are either coming off the ball—which is trying to pull the wrong pitches—or having trouble going the other way—which is getting jammed. So if you're trying to go up the middle, you can cover the whole plate. That way you're staying on the ball, hitting right back at the pitcher. You're not opening up, you're not trying to go the other way, you're just trying to hit it back at the pitcher. There are a lot of hits up the middle. And a lot of times I'll take that approach into the game and try to do just that.

CHAPTER 13

Situation Hitting

Baseball is a team game and a game of situations, and when you come to the plate, your job as a hitter will depend on any number of variables.

How many outs are there? How many runners are on base and who are they? What inning is it? What's the score? Who's coming to bat after you? Who's the pitcher? How is the defense positioned?

All these factors and more will influence how you approach your turn at bat. When you step into the batter's box, you have to have an idea of what you want to accomplish in that turn at bat as well as an idea of how you intend to do it.

Situation hitting is rooted in team play. A hitter who puts his own ego and achievements above the needs of the club in a given situation will not value situation hitting and will not be a team player. Such a player may wow the fans and impress the media, but he will not necessarily gain the respect and admiration of his teammates over the long haul. On the other hand, a player who understands situation hitting and is willing to do whatever it takes to help the team score runs might go unnoticed by the hero-worshiping public, but that player will often be highly esteemed by his teammates.

Situation hitting has two main laws: (1) when you come to bat with nobody on base, your job is to get on; (2) when you come to bat with a runner or runners on base, your job is to hit the ball to a part of the field where it is most likely to advance the runner or runners toward scoring.

With the bases empty, your job is to reach base safely. There are four ways you can do that: base hit, walk, error, hit by pitch.

The last is obviously the least desirable, but if you're facing a pitcher who doesn't throw particularly hard and you have a chance, on an inside pitch, to "take one for the team," why not? In that case, rolling will help you in one more way, because in order to be awarded first base, you have to make an effort to avoid getting hit, and rolling is enough.

Of the other three ways, two depend on making contact. There's not much to say about a base hit. It's obviously the most satisfying way for a hitter to get on. But reaching base on an error can be equally productive because committing an error has a demoralizing effect on the defensive team.

So does a walk, and that's why managers hate to see their pitchers give away free passes. Every batter should know the strike zone and be willing to work in order to draw a base on balls. With nobody on base, the old saying, "A walk's as good as a hit," is as true as ever.

With a runner or runners on base, your job becomes more complicated, but the basic rule is to always advance the runner. Sometimes the situation will call for a standard play, such as a hit and run or a sacrifice bunt. These situations will almost always be called for by your manager or coach.

The principle of advancing the runner doesn't necessarily mean giving yourself up. *Always try to hit the ball hard to get on base.* (If you're bunting, always think in terms of beating it out.) But advancing the runner may mean hitting to a certain part of the field.

Let's take a couple of examples.

Runner on first, nobody out. You have to hit the ball behind the runner, to the right of second base so the runner can at least get to third. Ideally you'll drive the ball to right field or right center for a hit and the runner on second will score. If you fly out

It's always important to know the strike zone.

to right field, the runner can tag up and advance. If the ball's hit on the ground, the runner can take off—if it gets through the infield, he scores, and if you ground out to the first or second baseman, he still advances. So even if you fly out or ground out to the right side, you've got a runner on third with only one out, and there are many ways to get that run home.

But if you hit the ball in front of the runner, to the left side of second, it has to be a base hit for the runner to advance. If it's on the ground, he has to wait until it's through the infield to run, which decreases his chances of scoring on the play. And if you fly out to left field, there's little chance that the runner can tag.

If the batter in front of you did his job and moved the runner along with a ground ball to second, you come to plate with a runner on third and one out. If it's early in the game, the first and third basemen will probably play in to try and cut down the run at the plate, but the second baseman and shortstop will usually play back. You have to hit the ball anywhere between ten feet to the left of the second baseman and ten feet to the right of the shortstop. If it's a fly ball, the runner can tag and come home. If it's a grounder, he can also score.

But if you pull the ball to one of the corners—to the third baseman if you're a righty, the first baseman if you're lefthanded—the runner is probably going to be thrown out at the plate.

One situation every batter faces is hitting with two strikes in the count. In this case, you have to protect the plate—with no strikes or one strike you try to hit within your high percentage zones, but with two strikes, you have to hit the umpire's strike zone. The rule of thumb here is to cut down on your swing a little and concentrate even more on contact. Perhaps choke up a bit for more bat control. Don't swing quite as hard, but still try to hit the ball hard up the middle.

Situation hitting requires thinking. The question you should always ask yourself is "What do I need to do to help my team score?" If there's nobody on base, you get on. If there's a runner or runners on base, hit the ball to the part of the field where it's most likely to advance them towards scoring.

What the hitters say

HAROLD BAINES Charlie Lau taught me a lot about situation hitting and what to look for. There are times when I go to the plate looking for a certain pitch, and I'll take two strikes if I don't get that pitch. With men in scoring position, the pitcher will usually try to stay away from my power, so I'm looking for a pitch on the outside part of the plate that I can drive into left field.

If it's later in the ballgame, I'll be looking for a certain pitch. After two at bats, I pretty much know how I'm going to be pitched the rest of the game.

I used to spread out my legs when I had two strikes and take a shorter, more compact swing. I don't do it anymore.

WADE BOGGS I don't make any adjustments for the count. I've always been able to make contact, and I've never had a fear of striking out.

ANDRE DAWSON I've been known to choke up with two strikes, so I have a little more bat control.

CARNEY LANSFORD I adjust my thinking at the plate depending on the situation. If I have two strikes, I'll choke up a little bit and shorten my swing. I just don't take as big or as hard a swing as normal—at least try to put the ball in play. Also, I'll widen my strike zone—you can't afford to take a pitch that might be just a little out of the strike zone.

RYNE SANDBERG When you're going up to hit, you have to have some idea of what you're going to try and do, according to what the situation might call for. It might call for hitting the ball the other way. You try to check the defense and see how they're positioning you. If I'm ahead in the count and I need to drive the ball, I might look in a certain zone inside and be ready to be quick inside. If it's not there, I take the pitch.

With two strikes, I try to cut down on my swing somewhat. Rather than driving the ball, I just want to put the ball in play with two strikes. Hit the ball where it's pitched. When you're hitting for power, you're very aggressive, and the swing is just a little bit harder. But with two strikes, I might shorten my stride a little bit. Some guys choke up on the bat, but I don't.

Brett Butler of the San Francisco Giants is regarded as one of the finest bunters in baseball.

CHAPTER 14

Bunting

Hall of Famer Harmon Killebrew, whose 573 lifetime home runs rank him fifth on the all-time list, had 8,147 at bats in his twenty-two-year big league career (1954-75), and he never once laid down a bunt. "I wish I had, just to keep the infield honest," says Killebrew today.

Killebrew's point is that since the first and third basemen knew he never bunted, they could always play him deep. If he'd occasionally dropped a bunt down, it would have had two effects. First, since they were positioned far back, he stood a good chance of beating out even a halfway decent bunt. Second, they would have had to at least consider the bunt possibility, and if they moved in a few steps to defend against that, it would have given him an advantage in shooting a hard ground ball through the infield.

Bunting is a skill that every player needs to have—the advantages of knowing how to bunt are numerous. It gives you one more weapon in your arsenal and makes you a more complete hitter. As any third baseman will tell you, fielding a well-placed bunt, on the run and barehanded, and throwing a runner out is no easy task. Many a time an infielder trying to rush a throw in such a situation will heave the ball past the first baseman, with the runner winding up on second or even third base.

You never know when you might have the opportunity to start a rally, move a runner along in a key situation, or even win a ballgame with a well-timed, well-executed bunt.

Against a pitcher you have trouble hitting, knowing how to bunt can mean the difference between 0 for 3 and 1 for 3 for the day. If you're a light hitter like San Francisco Giants outfielder Brett Butler, you can raise your batting average considerably by bunting for base hits. "The hardest thing for me on a baseball field has always been to hit," says Butler, who is considered by many to be the best bunter in the game today. "I could always run, and bunting just emphasized that. I make it a point of trying to bunt at least once in every game."

Even if you're a power hitter like Killebrew, whose intent is merely to "keep the infield honest" with an occasional surprise, you can only help yourself as a hitter by knowing how to bunt.

Mickey Mantle not only was a great power hitter, but was a great bunter from the left side of the plate.

There are two main styles of bunting.

One method is squaring toward the pitcher by bringing your back foot up parallel with your front one. This style is used more often when bunting for a sacrifice.

When you square, you have to get around in time to be balanced, but it's important not to square too early, or you'll tip off the infield. In sacrifice bunting it's better to bunt first and then run. You see the ball better, and you have much better bat control when you're not moving.

Keep in mind that when we talk about "sacrifice" we're not saying you should automatically give yourself up. In sacrifice bunting, your job is to move the runner along. The most important thing is to make certain that you get the ball down in a good area—the defense still has to throw you out. After you've put the ball in play, you're trying to get on base. If you run down the baseline, you put extra pressure on the infield to make the play, and that increases their chances of making an error.

The second style of bunting is keeping your feet as they are in your batting stance, but pivoting on your toes. This style is used more in bunting for a hit, although there are bunters who use it in a sacrifice situation as well.

In sacrifice bunting, you bunt the ball first and run second. When bunting for a hit, however, many of the great bunters get a little head start. The technique varies a bit, depending on whether you're a lefthanded or righthanded hitter.

A lefty who is dragging a bunt down the first base line or pushing one up the third base line will begin with a little crossover step to get a fast break out of the batter's box. Mickey Mantle, who was not only one of the greatest power switch-hitters in baseball history, but also one of the greatest drag bunters from the left side of the plate, used this type of running start.

A righthanded hitter bunting for a hit usually puts

The square style of bunting is used more in sacrificing.

The pivot style of bunting is more often used when bunting for a base hit, although some bunters use it in sacrificing as well.

A lefthanded hitter can use a crossover step for a fast start out of the batter's box.

A righthanded batter can drop his rear foot back for a fast start when bunting for a hit.

the ball down the third base line. He drops his rear foot back just before contact for a fast break out of the box.

"The main thing is where you put the ball," says Carney Lansford. "If you're bunting for a base hit down the third base line, you want to make it just barely fair. If you bunt the ball there, it's almost impossible for them to get you out. I know—I'm a third baseman."

In both methods of bunting, there are two principles that must be followed. First, you have to get the bat out in front of the plate—if you bunt with your bat behind the plate, you're in danger of fouling the ball off. Second, it's essential to stay balanced—knees bent and weight on the balls of your feet.

Your top hand slides up the bat about halfway or a little more. Some players encircle the bat with their fingers, which gives you greater control but also involves one big risk—if the ball hits your hand, you've got a couple of broken fingers. A better technique is to turn your hand in and cradle the bat with your thumb and forefinger.

Whichever method you use, the most important thing is for both hands to be loose, because you want to deaden the ball on impact, which won't happen if you're gripping the bat tightly. Try to make contact about three to five inches from the top end of the bat and have the bat parallel to the ground.

You determine the placement of your bunt by the angle of your bat to the pitch. Keep the ball away from the pitcher, who has the easiest play by far. Either force the third or first baseman to field the ball, or get it between the pitcher and one of those fielders, especially if the pitcher's follow-through carries him off the mound in one direction and opens up a space in the infield.

It's best not to bunt on a high pitch because of the danger of popping the ball up for an easy out or, worse yet, a double play. If the situation demands that you bunt and the pitch is high, be sure you get on top of the ball so you don't pop it up.

Practice your bunting consistently, and you will add another dimension to your hitting.

Make contact three to five inches from the end, with the bat parallel to the ground.

Encircling the bat with your hand gives you more control, but exposes your hand to possible injury if the ball hits it.

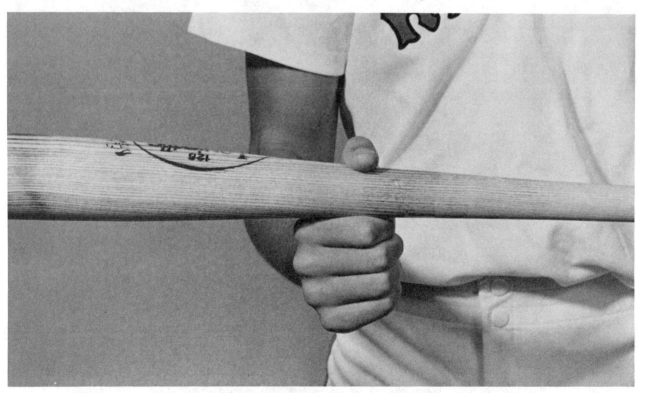

Turning your hand in and cradling the bat with your thumb and forefinger is a safer method.

Working with a batting tee gives you a chance to concentrate on mechanics and problem areas in the strike zone without having to find someone to pitch batting practice.

CHAPTER 15

Drills and Practice

There's nothing that will improve your hitting more than disciplined practice. Repetition is the most effective way to master the mechanics. You need to do this because when you step into the batter's box in a game, you want your body to react correctly by habit. A live at bat during a game is not the time to be experimenting, learning new techniques, or making changes in basics—that work is done during practice.

Besides batting practice against live pitching and pitching machines, there are several other drills that are quite helpful for working on your mechanics. *Remember, always wear a protective batting helmet when practicing.*

The first is using a batting tee. The two great benefits of hitting off a tee are that you can practice alone, and because the ball is not moving, you can focus on the mechanics of your swing while reducing all the other variables of hitting to a minimum.

With a tee, you can work on any part of the strike zone you may be having trouble with. If you're getting tied up by the high, inside pitch, put the ball there on the tee, take your normal stance, and figure out why you're not having success hitting pitches in that area. See what adjustments you need to make in order to increase your ability to handle those pitches. If you're having trouble getting your bat on the low, outside pitch, put the ball there and analyze the problem. It's a good idea to move the ball around the entire strike zone and work at hitting in all areas.

The second drill is the soft-toss. This exercise requires two people. The tosser stands about ten feet off to the side, and flips the ball out in front of the batter, who hits the ball into a net. Again, as with hitting off a tee, this drill is valuable for working on different areas of the strike zone, though the predictability of the ball's location is somewhat decreased by the human factor.

There are several other key aspects of hitting that are helped by the soft-toss drill. Weight shift, waiting on the ball, keeping your head down, and follow-through can all be improved through this drill. Soft-toss is a perfect drill for the batter who is having trouble getting his hips into his swing—in such a case, lifting the back heel and pivoting on the

The bottom hand drill is especially good for hitters who have a dominant top hand.

The soft-toss drill is excellent for two people.

back toe will automatically force the hips open.

There are a couple of variations of the soft-toss drill which are also excellent. The first is the bottom hand drill, in which the hitter swings with only the bottom hand on the bat. This is especially suited for hitters who tend to have a dominant top hand which rolls too soon and cuts off arm extension in the swing and follow-through.

The second variation of the soft-toss is for batters who bring their hands with them when they stride, thereby starting their swing too soon. In this drill, the hitter takes his stride, keeping his hands back, and only then does the tosser flip the ball.

Another drill that's excellent practice as well as great fun is the time-honored pastime of pepper. This brisk little game involves anywhere from two

to four fielders and one batter. The hitter usually chokes up five or six inches on the bat and the fielders stand about twenty feet away.

The object of the game for the fielders is to glove the batted ball and fire it back in the shortest possible time. The hitter gets to practice quick reactions, bat control, a compact swing, and following the ball all the way with his eyes. In addition, the hitter is required to hit line drives and ground balls, because a pop fly will carry over the fielders' heads and the game is held up while one of them has to chase the ball.

These drills will help you develop as a hitter. We've said it many times, but it bears repeating once more: *there are no shortcuts to becoming a good hitter, and there is no substitute for practice.*

Pepper is a good drill for practicing quick reactions, bat control, a compact swing, and following the ball all the way with your eyes.

What the coach says

DUSTY BAKER One of the things that's missing today—the earlier generations of players had extremely strong hands from working. Hank Aaron had hands like iron—he grew up working on an ice truck. We work on weights today, but not that much on hand strength. I try to get guys to work on hand strength. The stronger your hands, the quicker you can start your bat and the quicker you can stop it.

I see guys wind up with a grooved swing from batting cages. They go down to the cage to hit, and they stand in the same spot and hit the ball right down the middle of the plate over and over again. That's where the pitcher is taught *not* to throw. Okay, if he happens to throw it down the middle of the plate, you're going to kill it. When you go to the cage, move away from the plate and make everything outside. Then move onto the plate and make everything inside. That way you learn to get to the ball. Move up in the box to make your hands quicker. Move back in the box to teach yourself how to wait. It's the same with a batting tee—make it inside, outside, low, high. The same with batting practice.

What the hitters say

HAROLD BAINES You don't take batting practice just to take it. There's got to be a reason behind it. The way you practice is the way you're going to perform in the game. When I take batting practice, I try to work on hitting to all parts of the ballfield. I start with trying to hit to left field, then to left-center, and move around all the way to right field. I never start off trying to pull the ball. Always start the opposite way and work my way around.

WADE BOGGS I don't really work on anything in particular during batting practice. I just concentrate on hitting the ball hard every time. Batting practice is essential. It's the only way to get better. You can't just go out there and say you're ready for a game if you miss practice. During the off-season, practice is a major part of my preparation. Even during the regular season, I take extra batting practice just to stay sharp. My advice is to take as much batting practice as you can.

ANDRE DAWSON In batting practice, I try to hit several pitches to the opposite side. Stay behind the ball, see it a lot longer. Then I try to hit the ball up the middle. Then I'll pull the ball. The last four or five swings, I just take my natural cuts. Those are the things I like to work on because they're all basic, all fundamental baseball, and good hitters should be able to perform those when they're at their best. I don't get anything out of going into batting practice and trying to hit everything out of the ballpark, because you're not going to get the type of pitches to do that in the game.

I don't think you can ever really practice too much. I'd clarify that—I don't want to say "too long," because you can get tired and develop bad habits. I think you should practice every day. Hit off a tee, then take some cuts against pitching. I think it's important to have the right people working with you who are drilling you day in and day out, reminding you of flaws, and also of what you're doing right, so the right things sink in, and you don't repeat the same mistakes that you might if you didn't have the help.

Using a tee, you work on hand and wrist coordination. Also your stride. You can really stride into the ball and swing down through it and drive it, instead of lifting it, which can happen when you face a machine. Against a machine, you have a tendency to try and time it, and you get out in front with your stride.

You want to continually work on hand-eye coordination and bat speed. I like to stress bat speed, because with bat speed you can make up for a lot of mistakes. You can be fooled and still catch up. I recommend doing a lot of the soft toss drill to help you develop quick hands and bat speed. The quicker your hands are, the better. If I'm hitting off a machine, sometimes I'll move up in front of the plate, and not really stride. Just use my hands and try to hit it up the middle, then to right field, then try to turn on it.

It's important not to be afraid up at the plate. The main thing is believing in your ability, working day in and day out to get the best out of yourself. It all ties in together—I think the more you work, the more faith you have in your abilities. The harder you work, the better you become and the more successful you are.

DWIGHT EVANS It's all discipline. Repetition is part of that discipline. Over and over and over.

TONY GWYNN Consistency takes hard work and a little heart. If you want to be consistent, you'd better do the little things. Like take an extra 10 minutes of batting practice, or do a little bit of video work.

CARNEY LANSFORD In batting practice I try to work first of all on establishing that I can hit the ball the other way, to right field, right-center. I try to hit line drives. The last few swings of batting practice I'll go ahead and pull a few balls, but usually I like to get my swing down first, and when I'm swinging the bat well, I'm hitting the ball to right field a lot.

Batting practice is most important because however you practice, you take that into the game. Your work habits are the most important thing in anything you do, and especially in baseball, you have to have good work habits. Good work habits are the number one thing if you want to be a good hitter. A lot of people say that you're either born a good hitter or you're not. I think that with practice you can become anything you want. If you want to become a good hitter and you work hard enough at it, you can do it. You can make yourself a good hitter—a lot of players have.

RYNE SANDBERG I have my routine in batting practice. We get about four or five rounds. The first round I like to lay down three or four good bunts—two down first base, two down third. The next pitch I like to do a hit-and-run, no matter where the pitch is. That doesn't mean necessarily hitting the ball the other way—just

on the ground someplace. The next pitch I like to pretend there's a runner on second and nobody out, and get him over by hitting the ball the other way. I have five or six swings left in the first round, and I like to drive the ball the other way, into right field. I like to work on that stroke. I think it's the toughest stroke to have. The second two rounds I try to hit the ball where it's pitched and maybe pull the ball, too. The last two rounds I might go for a little more power.

Practice is very important. We practice every day during the season. We spend an hour on the field before every game, and we work on everything. In the middle of the season, if I were to miss a week of batting practice, I wouldn't feel the same at the plate. I think it's very important to use practice to work on your weaknesses. If you're a big, strong guy and you can pull the ball and hit it out of the park, I wouldn't use batting practice only to pull and hit the ball out. If I had problems with the pitch away, I'd like to see that pitch in batting practice and work on that.

SELECTED BIBLIOGRAPHY

Hriniak, Walt, with Henry Horenstein and Mark Starr. *A Hitting Clinic: The Walt Hriniak Way.* Harper & Row, N.Y. 1988.

Lau, Charlie, with Alfred Grossbrenner. *The Art of Hitting .300.* Hawthorn Books, N.Y. 1980.

Lau, Charlie. *The Winning Hitter: How to Play Championship Baseball.* Hearst Books, N.Y. 1984.

Ruth, George Herman. *Babe Ruth's Own Book of Baseball.* G.P. Putnam & Sons, N.Y. 1928.

Williams, Ted, and John Underwood. *The Science of Hitting.* Simon and Schuster, N.Y. 1970.

PHOTO CREDITS

The Babe Ruth Museum: p. 5.

National Baseball Library: p. 2 top left, bottom
left & right, 3, 10, 13-15 all, 22, 29 top left, bottom
left & right, 36, 50, 54, 69, 74, 76.

Courtesy San Francisco Giants: p. 26.

Courtesy Texas Rangers: p. 23.

TV Sports Mailbag: p. 2 top right, 12, 20, 29 top
right, 30 top right, 32, 68.

Cover photo by Tom DiPace.

All other photos by Mike Saporito.